Effective Internal Control Practices in Banks

Effective Internal Control Practices in Banks: A Practitioner's Aid

BY

SOPHIA BECKETT VELEZ

International Leadership Association (ILA), USA

emerald PUBLISHING

United Kingdom – North America – Japan – India – Malaysia – China

Emerald Publishing Limited
Emerald Publishing, Floor 5, Northspring, 21-23 Wellington Street, Leeds LS1 4DL

First edition 2025

British Library Cataloguing in Publication Data
A catalogue record for this book is available from the British Library

ISBN: 978-1-83662-973-3 (Print)
ISBN: 978-1-83662-972-6 (Online)
ISBN: 978-1-83662-974-0 (Epub)

Printed and bound by CPI Group (UK) Ltd, Croydon, CR0 4YY

To my daughter Shikurah Velez – you are my biggest cheerleader, and I am thankful for your love and support.

To Theolores Dawes (Tilly) my Godmother – thank you for believing in me. You are gone but not forgotten.

To Courtney Fisher – thank you for your support during the storm of my life.

To Geoffrey Reid (fondly referred to as Br. Reid) – thank you for being there as a support and taking all the calls.

To my lovely Aunt Rose Grant, Lucky Hill, St Mary, Jamaica – thank you for giving my dreams wings to fly. I love you dearly. You are gone but not forgotten.

To Mrs Henry, Goshen Primary School Lucky Hill, St Mary – thank you for believing in me.

To Kenrick Beckett (my dad) and Tullo T – thank you for listening and protecting the dreams of young people.

Contents

List of Figures and Tables

Chapter 5

Chapter 6

Chapter 7

About the Author

Sophia Beckett Velez, PhD, has worked for over 16 years as a Certified Public Accountant (CPA) with large banks providing consulting services. Her work experience has provided her with valuable background information on the banking industry in general. As a CPA, she worked for firms such as PricewaterhouseCoopers, where she performed financial audits, attestation services and risk management analysis of large banks. Many of the regulatory compliance problems noted during her review of the large banks required her to cultivate relationships with line of business managers and work with them to develop action plans and solutions to the issues noted. This has sparked her research interest in exploring the issues at hand in global banks.

Preface

This book discussed the implementation of effective internal control practices in banks and public companies. The US Government (House of Representative, Congress) saw the urgency to pass laws and governance principles that will remediate weaknesses in internal control, mitigate scandals and address failures in these publicly filed companies. The root causes of these companies' crises and failures when analyzed were linked to ineffective internal control environment, deficiencies, inadequacies in internal systems, fraudulent activities tied to various areas (financial reporting, accounting, auditing, corporate governance, oversight) within public companies and banks.

A qualitative e-Delphi study of 10 banking finance experts was convened to build consensus on internal control practices senior bank managers can implement that can be effective in reducing losses in banks. This book offers consensus on: (a) performance of periodic risk and controls assessment, (b) monthly/quarterly reporting over controls performance to include key performance/risk indicators, (c) strong governance and oversight committees, (d) timely reporting and escalation, (e) setting expectations for communication and reporting, (f) ensuring employees have time to recognize problems and follow procedures and not cut corners when they are under extreme pressured, (g) automation of manual processes that are prone to human errors, (h) establish priority training and (i) having a risk taxonomy. These considerations towards effective internal control practices may help reduce reporting inaccuracies, lack of timely reporting, information inappropriateness which have caused banks to incur significant losses, failure to mitigate risk timely, reputational damage and regulatory findings.

This book offers an original contribution to the field of banking that undergraduates, master's, PhD students, academics and researchers can use to gain a deeper understanding of internal control risks in banks/public companies and the use of effective internal control practices. This book will be the first to discuss consensus on effective internal control practices in banks. Sophia Beckett Velez, PhD, has over 16 years of experience as a Certified Public Accountant (CPA), providing consulting services to large banks.

Sophia Beckett Velez

Acknowledgement

This book could not have been written without the support and encouragement of my daughter, Shikurah Velez.

Introduction

This book is divided into three parts. Part 1 discusses *Lack of Effective Internal Controls in Banks and Significant Financial Institutions (SIFIs)*. Part 2 examines *Government SOX Regulations of Banks and SIFIs Control Environment.* Part 3 discusses *Bank Leadership Consensus on Designing Effective Control Environment.*

Part 1: Lack of Effective Internal Controls in Banks and Significant Financial Institutions (SIFIs)

This part of the book discusses bank failures due to ineffective internal controls, related significant losses incurred. The impacts of weak internal controls on financial reporting, accounting, auditing, corporate governance, oversight. The role of Board of Directors in control weakness and the passing of Sarbanes Oxley Act 2002.

Chapter 1: Banks and SIFIs Failure to Implement Effective Internal Controls

In this chapter, I discuss the root causes of banks and public companies' crises and failures that are linked to ineffective internal control environment, deficiencies, inadequacies in internal systems, fraudulent activities tied to various areas (financial reporting, accounting, auditing, corporate governance, oversight) of these organizations. The ineffective control environment at these companies led to millions in Federal regulator fines and banks found guilty of creating millions of fake accounts in the name of customers without their consent; this resulted in the firing of employees.

Chapter 2: Significant Losses Incurred by Large Banks and SIFIs Due to Internal Control Weaknesses

Several large global banks failures before and after the 2008 financial crises that had ineffective internal control systems due to poor governance and board oversight are discussed. Global banks significant losses from fraudulent actions occurrence due to weak internal controls that did not prevent these fraud events are examined. The importance of internal controls in relation to losses in large companies and banks and the shock to the global economy/financial sector. Board of directors' failure to do their duties in protecting the company from fraud, senior management abuse of power and lack of risk mitigation through enforcement of good governance and controls.

Chapter 3: Global Economic Impact Due to Weak Controls in Banking and Financial Services

This part of the book discusses large banks' significant losses and exposure to insolvency due to weak internal control environment, non-functioning internal controls and government rescue to mitigate the insolvency that would be a systemic risk to global financial structure. Central banks widening their focus from providing banks liquidity insurance, to backstopping market liquidity in scenarios where severe dysfunction threatens the banks financial stability. Mitigation of dysfunctional banking environment and fostering stability, quelling the fears of customer in the markets.

Chapter 4: Sarbanes Oxley 2002 (SOX) and Control Environment

The US Government's passage of laws to mitigate internal control risk in public companies are examined. The US and global governments who followed suit believed that there is a lack of effective functioning internal controls within public traded companies control environment which caused them to go out of business. Several major corporate and accounting scandals and the related effects on investors' confidence, incurrence of losses in billions of dollars when the share prices of the impacted companies collapsed and consumers developed negative public confidence in financial securities markets are reviewed. This need for SOX controls, hearings held by the Senate Banking Committee on the market problems that constituted losses of billions, spiralling of trillions of dollars in market value losses, and the passing of Sarbanes–Oxley Act of 2002.

Part 2: Government SOX Regulations of Banks and SIFIs Control Environment

The US and global government passage of laws to mitigate internal control weakness and systemic impact globally. The challenges to the implementation of SOX are discussed. Stakeholders' failures in implementing SOX effectively are examined.

Chapter 5: Importance of Effective Internal Control to Company's Control Environment

This chapter discusses analysis of internal control risk in their accounting practices as part of their approach to implement improved risk control measures. The initiative of mitigating risk carried out in concert with daily management and operations. The importance of an effective internal control environment and the requirements to prevent, detect and monitor corporate misconduct, information asymmetry, moral hazard, mortgage fraud, predatory lending, managerial slack and risk shifting.

Chapter 6: Challenges to the Effective Implementation of SOX Requirements

Companies' actions that challenge the implementation of SOX are discussed. The sending of lobbyist to Washington to kill the SOX 2002 bill. The complains at first launch that the bill is over regulation of firms that were required to be compliant with Section 404(b) of the Act, which addresses reporting on company's internal controls. Lobbyist attack Fed measures to mitigate internal control weaknesses to prevent fraud, management misconduct and possibility of being discontinued.

Chapter 7: Regulators, Auditors and Process Owners Failures in SOX Certification Process

This chapter discusses stakeholders who faced challenges and failures in executing SOX guidelines resulting in payment of penalties and findings for non-compliance. External audit firms are required to perform audit of the public company financial report and internal controls. The findings brought against external audit firms' failure to challenge or question missing disclosures relating to significant debt of companies they audited.

Chapter 8: Internal Control Framework (Preventive, Detective, Monitoring, Automated) Design

This chapter discusses the design of the control environment consistent of structures, methods and measures that are foundational in the evaluation of the internal control framework. The framework/design of internal controls system inclusion of foundational pieces such as control environment, risk assessment, control activities, information and communication and monitoring. Internal control activities design and operating effectiveness are relevant to maintain a sustainable system with a mixture of manual and automated.

Part 3: Bank Leadership Consensus on Designing Effective Control Environment

This part of the book discusses effective internal control environment. The use of automated controls, risk identification process, effective communication, timely reporting and escalation.

Chapter 9: Systems and the Automated Control Environment

A well-designed internal control environment and the automation of many of its control activities and processes are examined. The less manual reliance a process is in its operation, the lower the risk of errors and fraud. A review and examination of bank systems, effective controls around its accounting business and the lack of system controls that contribute to system risk is reviewed.

Chapter 10: Risk Identification and Communication

Banks and public companies' risk identification processes are discussed and their exposure to risk domestically and globally stemming from the business environment in which they execute their transactions. The nature of goods and services, individuals executing the processes, laws and regulations that governs these activities and the technology/system used to carry out these business events are examined. Banks' analysis of these varied factors of risk is embedded in transactions and the risk identification process used to identify the What Can Go Wrong in the execution of its business activities.

Chapter 11: Timely Reporting and Escalation

This chapter discusses the needs and impacts on the companies' financial health when timely information is shared through communication channels such as reporting, assessments and audit results. The crucial role timely reporting and escalation play in various stakeholders being able to react and take responsive measures to prevent identified issues from progressing materially.

Chapter 12: Internal Control Effective Practices

This chapter examines significant positive impacts effective internal control play in the maintenance of a strong bank's control environment. This is reflected in its risk management programmes, financial reporting, oversight committees, meeting regulatory requirements and the overall profitability of the organization. The internal control consensus activities are discussed and the efforts to mitigate control risk.

Part 1

Lack of Effective Internal Controls in Banks and Significant Financial Institutions (SIFIs)

Chapter 1

Banks' and SIFIs' Failure to Implement Effective Internal Controls

Significant Financial Institutions (SIFIs) are large institutions such as banks, insurance companies and public corporations that have major financial impacts on domestic and global economies. The nature of SIFI institutions caused the Federal Reserve Bank (Fed) to roll out risk management requirements, capital stress test for designated entities, tools to identify and manage risks and losses (Allen et al., 2016). Capital stress test is a complex process which makes risk management effort very challenging as a tool used to address risk (Allen et al., 2016). The nature of the risk in the financial markets stems from financial distress SIFIs, which hinders management to achieve financial stability and control systemic risk (Allen et al., 2016). There are trade-off in the risk mitigation efforts noted by Allen et al. (2016) that these efforts stifle financial innovations, and it is unclear how to design an effective regulatory framework. Significant losses if left unmitigated can lead to banks facing insolvency. These companies' losses contributed to business failures and global financial crisis. Aksoy and Mohammed (2020) asserts global banks experienced crises and failures which resulted in their insolvency; this had negative impacts to global investor confidence. The root causes of these companies' crises and failures when analysed were linked to ineffective internal control environment, deficiencies, inadequacies in internal systems, fraudulent activities tied to various areas (financial reporting, accounting, auditing, corporate governance, oversight) of the company (Aksoy & Mohammed, 2020). Board of Directors (BOD) sets the tone and temperature of the internal control environment through their company policies; this influences the procedures and controls used to conduct daily transactions and operations. Goldberg (2017) argues that banks and SIFI institutions are required to have controls, compliance policies and procedures, that should be reflected in the execution of the organization operations.

The banks' BOD can provide oversight over the companies' policies and procedures, through controls designed to carry out sound business initiatives, incentive and organizational structure of the bank. Equally important to organizational structure is the BOD structure which can be an impediment to timely response to a

Effective Internal Control Practices in Banks, 3–14

doi:10.1108/978-1-83662-972-620251001

bank suffering significant losses and the possibility of insolvency. O'Sullivan et al. (2016) contend that when a bank has a large board with several members, this can be a hindrance to them making timely risk management decision for a bank that is in crisis. An effective control environment is one where there is an examination of the board structure, CEO and board tenure, prior to a crisis (O'Sullivan et al., 2016). There is a direct relation between an effective board design and the increase in bank performance (O'Sullivan et al., 2016). When there is a lack of effective and positive BOD involvement and oversight, it shows up in senior management abusive conduct, fraud, resulting in fines to the company from regulator for lack of compliance with the rules and regulations. Tourigny et al. (2003) assert management behaviour that lacks principles of governance and ethical standards can lead to bank failures (Tourigny et al., 2003). This gap in governance can be mitigated through the nurturing of ethical leadership evident in leaders' activities (champion of moral and integrity, display ethical behaviour) which is reflected in their product choices (Lui, 2011). Bank managers who lack morals and ethics, pursue their own financial gains which exposed shareholders to significant losses (Lui, 2011).

The ineffective control environment at Wells Fargo Banks led to Federal regulator imposing a $185 million fine on the bank for creating millions of fake accounts in the name of customers without their consent; this resulted in the firing of 5,000 employees (Aksoy & Mohammed, 2020). Well Fargo Bank leadership's lack of ethical practices led to them fraudulently creating accounts to fill sales quota. Bank managers goals and practices used to execute the daily activities of the company can be found in goal theory; Additionally, the incentives that motivated the aspirations of the agents are embedded in goal theory (Chawla, 2016). Chawla (2016) posits companies used their commission plans to motivate individual to reach sales target goal. Many organizations that have implemented rewards and punishment strategy to motivate salespeople had some backlash where some of the employees became disengaged salesperson; this caused reputational damage to the organization (Chawla, 2016). Some extrinsic motivational methods can yield negative results, fraudulent behaviour, and expose the banks to significant systemic losses. Preventive measures can be implemented by the bank to mitigate widespread fraudulent acts; this entails implementing practices that inform bank managers positive actions through ethical choices awareness (Gatzert & Schmit, 2016). The continuous increase of significant losses in mega banks which spill over into the economy causing turmoil, suggests the lack of effective internal company controls (Tanda, 2015). There are increases in bank risks driven by managers' aggressive lending activity that turned out to be bad loans and failed financial innovation that contributed to significant losses that eroded the economy (Egly et al., 2016). Senior bank managers' behaviours that increase bank risk can be mitigated through the use of risk management practices. Bank managers need to be trained to make conservative investment selections that would increase company profits, reduce fraudulent behaviour and minimise business losses (Gatzert & Schmit, 2016).

Pakistan had banks that lack effective control environment which was tied to wrongful issuances of debit card and chequebook on customer accounts; this allowed the perpetrators to misuse and make unauthorized withdrawals from the accounts (Abdullah et al., 2018). The internal control weakness at a Pakistan branch in Peshwar City was manipulated by an employee of 5 years who used the three key account characteristics (accounts with significant number of deposits, easy specimen signatures, fewer inquiries made by owners of these accounts) to select accounts to commit fraud (Abdullah et al., 2018). The fraudulent acts committed by employees at the Pakistan bank include obtaining illegal cards and using supplementary debit card with a daily withdrawal limit of Rs. 25,000 to make unauthorized withdrawals, issuing and using chequebook by faking the specimen signature repeatedly for personal use (Abdullah et al., 2018). In the United States, there were numerous banks that issued bad loans which generated significant losses linked to weak risk management environment manipulated by originators and arrangers (Lui, 2011). Some banks conducted subprime lending which caused significant losses; this includes government-sponsored enterprises (Freddie Mac, Fannie Mae) who had liabilities of $5 trillion, and $2 trillion of subprime mortgages losses (Allison, 2017). These significant losses and failures in subprime lending in banks continued to increase over time because of policies that gradually decayed by the actions of the Fed (Hanke & Sekyere, 2017). The Fed guaranteed loans offered by Fannie Mae and Freddie Mac which allowed these banks to take on more risk; this incentivised growth in bad mortgage lending to unqualified customers (Hanke & Sekerke, 2017). Banks in the United States continues to operate at a high risk of insolvency due to low levels of (leverage, liquidity, capital) and lack of effective control to curtail senior bank managers' risky behaviour (Dandapani et al., 2017). Gastón and Schumacher (2017) assert regulations that address liquidity levels can decrease the probabilities of default for banks, prevent the default risk during a crisis episode and improve the financial soundness of the banking sector.

The US banks continue to have significantly high debt to equity ratios, lower liquidity and capital adequacy ratios and take on bad home mortgage lending which experienced default (Dandapani et al., 2017). Large banks labelled as SIFI (Citigroup, Goldman Sachs, JPMorgan Chase, Morgan Stanley, Wells Fargo) in the United States continue to incur significant losses and high operational risk exposure (Sarin & Summers, 2016). Banks are faced with the challenge of meeting shareholder profit objectives which managers undertake by increased investments in high-risk products that provide short-term profits, while in the long term, these positions incurred significant bank losses (Sarin & Summers, 2016). Banks were interested in raking in higher profits and increased revenue from joint banking and insurance products, and they never focused on cutting costs (Yuan, 2017). Many banks' strategy to stay profitable and afloat was not aligned with sound internal control framework linked to organizational objectives. The Fed carried out stress test on significant banks in the United States which revealed many of them were under-capitalised. This means many of these banks' capital was insufficient to cover potential significant losses; Bank of America was one of the banks the Fed required to raise new capital and resubmit plans in 2015 (Walker et al., 2017).

This recommendation from the Fed caused Bank of America to spend $100 million to make internal improvement and resubmit its 2015 plan (Walker et al., 2017). Similarly, Citigroup spent $180 million in 2014 on submission of its plan to the Fed (Walker et al., 2017). Morgan Stanley resubmitted a revised capital plan for 2016 to the Fed, and some banks were penalised by the Fed for falling the stress test (Walker et al., 2017). Both Deutsche Bank and Santander US failed the tests and were penalised by the Fed who took actions which include prohibiting them from paying dividends and stock buybacks (Walker et al., 2017). The Fed should require banks to recapitalise following an adverse shock, raise equity capital and take actions to improve their capital ratios (Greenwood et al., 2017). Banks' maintenance of minimum capital ratios is appropriate for normal times, inadequate in the wake of a large negative shock in the system, but not appropriate during times of financial crisis (Greenwood et al., 2017). Banks' and it's subsidiaries have positive relationships during normal years when the economy is stable, negative relationship during crisis (Gregory & Hambusch, 2015). The capital-to-asset ratio has a negative relationship with bank risk; there should be an increase in capital ratio levels that help banks to mitigate negative crisis impacts (Gregory & Hambusch, 2015). The regulators have placed restrictions on buyback because of banks' adverse scenario results and have placed monitoring controls requirement guidelines around capital inflows and outflows in loan, trading losses, reserves balances, asset growth, revenues, income impact on the bank's balance sheet (Baker et al., 2017). Additionally, the Fed has placed restriction on dividends and share issuances for banks that had scenario results that were unfavourable (Baker et al., 2017).

Additionally, there is the risk that shadow banks posed to the banking sector and the economy that needs to be managed by the Fed. Federal regulators in the United States have gaps in their risk mitigation measures; they fail to manage risk posed by the shadow-banking system (Herr, 2016). Additionally, the relationships between commercial banks and the shadow-banking system should be regulated (Herr, 2016). Shadow banks were branded as an institution incentivised into being by the Fed and new regulations. Capital regulation caused more regulatory arbitrage and was linked to a large migration of traditional banking activities towards shadow-banking activities (Lin et al., 2018). However, Deos et al. (2015) have skepticism around Basel III regulation effectiveness; bankers were incentivized to migrate to shadow-banking activities to generate more profits, and lower-cost operations. Nisha (2016) warns too much regulation on banks can cause their managers to engage in more risky behaviour to generate profits. Banks with strong parent and subsidiaries tend to be engaged in risky activities and high-risk projects with problematic performances (Bressan, 2017). The banks tend to issue more subordinated debt securities, pay high interest and incur high funding cost (Bressan, 2017). Interest rate shocks have been used as a tool to identify monetary policy issues by the regulators to determine the relationship between capital requirements and aggregate risk in the market (Aliaga-Díaz & Olivero, 2012). Banks have to take turns in their recapitalise activities to ease the burden/stress on the economy that all of them capitalising at the same time would result in negative impacts (Aliaga-Díaz & Olivero, 2012). This could cause a reduction in bank credit, have negative impacts on investment and promote bank dependency (Aliaga-Díaz & Olivero, 2012). The parent company of a bank tends to assume higher shares/percentage of nonperforming loan, decline in the corporate liquidity, which erodes the financial condition of the banking groups (Bressan, 2017). The parent company of the subsidiary bank offers them support, increase commitment, and take on more of their substantial debt (Bressan, 2017). Erten and Ocampo (2017) mentioned there are countries that capital inflow surges during post-crisis recovery have been positive. Capital inflow/outflow and foreign exchange regulation coupled with financial sector restrictions have been effective in the reduction of foreign exchange pressures and real exchange rate appreciation as a result of large capital inflow (Erten & Ocampo, 2017). These markets' structures have positive effects on profits and competition with low risk (Mcmillan & Mcmillan, 2016). However, it should be noted that increased merger and market share concentration increase banks' risk reflected in their Z-score (Mcmillan & Mcmillan, 2016).

On the other hand, US regulators have issued guidelines relating to internal control activities banks are required to implement to ensure they maintain Tier 1 capital of 4 % of average consolidated on-balance-sheet assets (Herring, 2016). Banks have control activities that reviews the accuracy of the computation of supplementary leverage ratio calibrated against on-balance-sheet assets and off-balance-sheet exposures (Herring, 2016). Paulet (2016) mentioned the Fed requires banks to hold high-quality liquid assets subject to monitoring controls to mitigate their risk. Bank Tier 1 capital ratio requirements suggest they should choose between increasing their lending margins and reducing their risk-weighted assets (Paulet, 2016). Fed requires banks to use equity to meet their funding needs and less debt which should not impact value of the banks negatively and their overall cost of funding (Masera & Mazzoni, 2016). Banks have to establish controls that test revenue and losses projections, residential mortgages, trading revenue and capital ratios (Allen et al., 2016). Banks have designed models to perform stress test and scenario analysis, but these measures have set backs because of some of the inaccuracies in their predictions (Baradaran, 2014). These stress tests were unable to predict market risk and losses which have been seen as a potential risk to the banking sector (Baradaran, 2014).

Large banks that incurred significant losses without adequate capital could become insolvent which the Fed and central try to mitigate by providing bailout funds to the troubled bank they deemed too big to fail. Labonte (2013) asserts banks that are too big to fail can negatively impact the global financial system because of their size and interconnectedness. This protection that government provides to too big to fail banks that have significant losses was abused by bank managers and saw it as an incentive for them to undertake risky investments (Labonte, 2013). Taxpayers believe that government bailouts of banks are a burden to the public and citizens are not in full support of this tool used to rescue troubled banks. Davies (2015) offered an alternative approach to bailouts which is known as bail-in which could probably reduce the costs passed to the taxpayer by the Fed when they rescue the financial system. This alternative bail in method would impose costs on long-term creditors of the bank (Davies, 2015). These social welfare costs should be paid by the ultimate investors in bail-in bonds (pensioners and long-term savers) rather should not the paid by taxpayers (Davies, 2015). Government in the United States has sought to integrate macroprudential regulations with monetary policy as a solution in time of financial crisis (Redo, 2015). In periods where the economy is robust, government would restrict monetary policy, weaken the risk-taking tendency and inflation pressure, and resolved to tightened monetary policy during deflation (Redo, 2015). In order for regulators to effectively create laws and guidelines to prevent and curtail wreck less and fraudulent behaviours, they need to understand the root causes of the issues, roll out strategies and guidelines to mitigate these activities (Viljanen, 2016). Across the pond in Europe, weak internal controls in banks created an atmosphere where there were significant number of money laundering activities. The lack of effective measures to combat and prevent money laundering caused HSBC (Europe) to pay $1.9b fines in 2012 and US Bancorp $613m in 2018 (Aksoy & Mohammed, 2020). The United Kingdom (UK) incurred significant losses from scandals linked to JP Morgan losses in currency default swap markets that were substantial amount to the tune of over $6 billion in losses, $1 billion in fines from the London Whale scandal (Handorf, 2017).

Ghana banking sector was hit with scandals which included Bank for Housing and construction and Ghana Co-operative Bank failures in 2000s which the Ghanian government attempted to bailout by injecting a lump sum of Ghs 1.25m to liquidate both banks (Aksoy & Mohammed, 2020). Shi and Wang (2014) noted banks are exposed to internal control risk in their accounting processes due to lack of internal control supervision system and restraint measures in banks. Several banks and public companies incurred significant losses and fines from respective government bodies due to high internal control risk which is linked to a weak internal control environment. Public companies that trade on the stock markets (NASDAQ, NYSE) have high internal control risk when they have ineffective controls; this risk can cause harm to company's image as a publicly traded company resulting in losses to the company and affiliates reflected in their bottom-line results. Banks should manage their trade risk by implementing controls that support higher trade openness, decrease bank risk through the information provided, diversified their lending activities which can decrease overall bank risk (Badar et al., 2017). The practice of higher trade openness provides international diversification opportunities and reduce banks domestic concentration by opening up other alternative markets, which can decrease the impact of domestic financial crisis on bank risk (Badar et al., 2017). Toshiba negative news as noted by Hideaki and Naoki (2021) was scandalous and impacted the company's image which caused stock prices of Toshiba's lenders to decline because of the announcement of the accounting scandals.

Moreover, the banking industry is plagued with international cyber hacker heist which affected banks in Bangladesh. Chowdhury (2021) asserts Bangladesh Bank (Central Bank of Bangladesh) loss BDT 6796 million from the treasury account in 2016 linked to cyber hacking. A subsequent investigation revealed Farmers Bank embezzled BDT 5000 million with the assistance of 11 different companies from 2013 to 2017 (Chowdhury, 2021). Additionally, Janata Bank loan scam of BDT 12300 million during 2013–16, The corrupt company, NRB Commercial Bank did misdeeds in loan sanctioned of BDT 7010 million during 2013–16, BASIC Bank Embezzled BDT 45000 million using fictitious companies and doubtful accounts during 2009–2013, Bismillah Group obtain fraudulent loans of BDT 11,740 million from banks in 2011 in fake names and name and laundered the money to foreign countries (Chowdhury, 2021). These corruptions that took place over several decades paralysed the banking sector, and people lost confidence in the banking system of Bangladesh (Chowdhury, 2021). In order to reduce internal control risk, banks should focus on implementing and sustaining an effective internal control environment. An effective internal control environment deters high risk behaviour in bank employees and management. Chen et al. (2023) posit internal control environment of a company incentivise individuals to violate regulation if the business operates in a weak internal control environment. Companies tend to comply with regulation when they function in an effective and strong internal control environment. To mitigate/lower risk, an effective internal control environment is needed to reduce corporate misconduct; the sustainability of this environment can be achieved in a systematic approach, one that is complete, rigorous with quick-responding internal control system (ICSs) (Chen, Zhu & Wang, 2023). Ineffective ICSs is one of the most significant contributing factors in banking failures when they are unable to mitigate and control bank management high-risk decisions and potential threats the company faces (Hamed, 2023). The ICS systems are part of the established rules publicly traded global companies abide by when transacting their goods and services within the financial system.

A financial system is a group of institutions (banks, insurance companies, stock exchanges) that exist domestically and globally which facilitate the exchange of funds to finance projects (consumption, a return on their financial assets) for various purposes (Bezo & Dibra, 2023). The financial system layout established rules and practices borrowers and lenders abide by when executing transaction with each other and these rules stipulated projects execution activities (which ones get financed, who finances, terms of financial deals) and overall governance of these projects (Bezo & Dibra, 2023). Internal control is a very complex and difficult process, interpretation and execution of ICS varies by countries as noted in their varied traditional methods, techniques and philosophies exhibited in the implementation (Bezo & Dibra, 2023). The ICS process is implemented and maintained by the company's BOD, senior management/other employees to meet the objective of providing reasonable assurance regarding the achievement of effectiveness and efficiency of operations, reliable financial reporting information, achieving compliance requirement with applicable laws/regulations and safeguarding of assets (Hamed, 2023).

BOD and Audit Committees (AC) play active roles as stake holders in monitoring the ICSs and control environment. The BOD helps establish policies that govern the procedures and the reporting measures used to provide feedback to them and AC. The ICS meets the objectives of the BOD in the policy by fulfiling its role in assisting the Accounting Information System (AIS) of the organisation carry out its own role in tracking the flow of operational and financial transactions. Baker et al. (2023) mentioned ICS objective in a bank is to ensure that the companies' operational goals and performance are met and facilitate the smooth functioning of AIS. It is relevant to have effective internal controls on AIS to prevent banks from being susceptible to fraud (Baker et al., 2023). AIS is information technology-based solution that supports the control of the banks economic, financial operation and tracks the flow of inbound and outbound funds/

transactions (Baker et al., 2023). This information is kept in meaningful format for ready use by decision-makers. The bank's decision-makers obtain relevant information from the AIS for business strategy and decision-making in assisting the company meet its targets and goals (Baker et al., 2023).

In the US board structures monitors, the corporate accounting processes are oftentimes independent of AC (Hideaki & Naoki, 2021). Publicly traded companies on NYSE and NASDAQ listing rules do not require the BOD members to be from outside the organization, neither is this required by creditors or shareholders (Hideaki & Naoki, 2021). The key ICS components (control environment, risk assessment, control activities, information and communication, monitoring) are articulated in the Committee of Sponsoring Organizations of the Treadway Commission (COSO)'s 2013 framework (Hamed, 2023). Equally, Al-Hawatmeh (2021) contends internal controls success is based on its design which entails five elements (control environment, risk assessment, control activities, information and communication and monitoring). The failure of ICS systems in companies such as Enron and WorldCom have led to their demise. Enron and WorldCom had multiple antennae's that reach many industry sectors, and their failures caused negative domino effects on related and interrelated industries and companies worldwide. WorldCom and Enron failures were linked to weakness in the ICS and disabled crosschecks (Aksoy & Mohammed, 2020). Al-Matari et al. (2017) mentioned failures and crises in companies (Enron, Global Crossing, Tyco, World Com) have caused corporate scandals which have negatively impacted investor confidence resulted in these firms struggling to raise alternative capital from the stock market. Likewise, Hideaki and Naoki (2021) pointed to scandals relating to Enron and WorldCom which caused damages to investors' confidence in US capital markets; the recent accounting scandals in big corporations have increased doubts and lack of trust on relying on the quality of reported earnings for publicly traded companies.

Most recent significant accounting fraud scandals at Olympus Corp. and Toshiba Corp have caused Japanese internal governance systems to be widely criticised (Hideaki & Naoki, 2021). Similarly, Hideaki and Naoki (2021) mentioned opportunistic earnings was one of the main motivational factors behind Olympus Corp. and Toshiba Corp accounting scandal and suggested mitigation measures should addressed the root causes by focusing on opportunistic earnings management. Public companies have separated the various department/stakeholders and functions where there is separation of ownership and control which have incentivised managers' manipulation of earnings to maximize their own interests and influence the earnings information (Hideaki & Naoki, 2021). This self-interest practiced by managers ahead of meeting shareholders objective has been area of concern in the banking industry. There have been conflicts between bank shareholders and managers in relation to when is the appropriate timing to adopt financial innovations while balancing shareholder pressure to improve performances (Forrer & Forrer, 2015). Lui (2011) mentioned bank managers sometimes pursue their own financial gain interest and neglect shareholders interest which results in losses for the shareholders is an aspect of principal–agent theory. Sepdiningtyas and Santoso (2017) mentioned goal theory is another underlining cause of managers pursuing their own financial gains while exposing shareholders to losses; these behaviours are driven by intrinsic and extrinsic motivation factors embedded in goal theory have led to dysfunctional behaviours. Hideaki and Naoki (2021) referred to measures in Agency theory that highlights effective monitoring mechanisms that can address agency problems through the use of boards of directors and audit committees working together. The use of effective monitoring systems can mitigate the risk of opportunistic/ self-serving behaviours of managers. Hideaki and Naoki (2021) mentioned credible and reliable accounting earnings from companies can happened when the opportunistic behaviour of managers is restrained/prevented through various monitoring systems.

The US government (House of Representatives and the Senate) saw the urgency to look at laws and governing principles that address weaknesses in internal control and mitigate root causes of failures in these companies. The scandal stemming from the failure of Enron motivated US governmental bodies to place emphasis on passing laws that would regulate the effectiveness of internal controls which manifested in the passing of Sarbanes–Oxley Act (SOX) of 2002 (Aksoy & Mohammed, 2020). The root causes of the scandal noted by US Congress is the lack of effective ICSs which the SOX Act seeks to highlight remediation measures that will improve the internal control environment (Aksoy & Mohammed, 2020). There are other areas of weaknesses Congress noted that led to failures and scandals in these large companies namely, intentional damage and violation of ethical principles (integrity, honesty, transparency, independence accountability) that SOX aims to remediate (Aksoy & Mohammed, 2020). Companies with effective internal control apparatuses tend to have fair financial reporting (Hideakin & Naoki, 2021). Equally (Hamed, 2023) pointed to ICS compliance has positive impacts on banks and their financial sustainability. The monitoring sections of ICS, use of control activities, information and communication are key drivers of bank positive performance (Hamed, 2023). Shi and Wang (2014) mentioned in striving to perfect the ICS and mitigate bank accounting internal control risk effectively consideration should be given to the establishment of risk management responsibility system and improvements to employee's assessment. ICS has gained significant important because of the lessons learnt from the scandals and the passing of SOX laws in the United States to mitigate crises and business failures tied to the scandals (Aksoy & Mohammed, 2020). ICS global awareness underscore it as a safety measure in large global companies in protecting stakeholder interest, meeting companies' goals, corporate governance, quality assurance, corporate risk management (CRM), transparency, accuracy, accountability, sustainability and competitive advantage (Aksoy & Mohammed, 2020). SOX laws had knock on effects on globalisation, rapid change, technological developments, complexity which underscored the importance of ICS system operating effective internal controls as a critical element of the business ecosystem and business sectors (Aksoy & Mohammed, 2020).

In a prior study conducted by Sophia Velez PhD to identify effective internal control practices in banks, a qualitative e-Delphi study was used to build consensus among 10 banking finance experts across the United States on how to recognize senior manager's effective internal control practices in large banks. Purposive sampling was employed to solicit participants to form a panel with experience in the underlining study constructs. They were recruited via social media (LinkedIn groups) because of their background in banking and knowledge on the subject. The inclusion criteria for selecting the panel of experts for the e-Delphi study is as follows: (1) adult over the age of 18; (2) employed a minimum of 10 years in the banking industry; (3) possession of an MBA in Finance; and (4) currently employed as a consultant to a large bank in the United States. The conceptual framework for the study employs Compliance and Ethics Group's. principal-agent theory, and goal theory as lens to examine the extant literature and survey statement/responses (Velez, 2020). Compliance and Ethics Group's (OCEG) combines governance, risk management, internal control, assurance and compliance tools to enhance effectiveness and efficiency practices (Bezzina et al., 2014). The internal control research question (Velez, 2020) was:

- Describe internal control activities senior bank managers can implement towards capital regulation that can be effective in reducing losses in bank holding companies.

The experts were asked to rate each statement on the second-round questionnaire against two separate (desirability and feasibility) 5-point Likert scales. Desirability measure ranged from (1) highly undesirable to (5) highly desirable, and feasibility ranged from (1) definitely infeasible to (5) definitely feasible.

The second-round questionnaire included the following meaning of each item on the desirability scale:

- (1) – Highly undesirable: Will have major negative effect.
- (2) – Undesirable: Will have a negative effect with little or no positive effect.
- (3) – Neither desirable nor undesirable: Will have equal positive and negative effects.
- (4) – Desirable: Will have a positive effect with minimum negative effects.
- (5) – Highly desirable: Will have a positive effect and little or no negative effect.

The second-round questionnaire included the meaning of each item on the feasibility scale:

- (1) – Definitely infeasible: Cannot be implemented (unworkable).
- (2) – Probably infeasible: Some indication this cannot be implemented.
- (3) – May or may not be feasible: Contradictory evidence this can be implemented.
- (4) – Probably feasible: Some indication this can be implemented.
- (5) – Definitely feasible: Can be implemented.

The Round 1 results relating to Internal Control practices generated 33 statements. The panel of expert's recommendations for Internal Control in the first-round questionnaire 33 statements were used in the second round of the questionnaire aligned to the following subcategories: Reporting, Timely Monthly/Quarterly Reporting, Data Management, Utilization of Loss Databases, Risk Management Oversight, Change Management and Self-Assessment, Prioritise Training, Governance Oversight, Committees and Line of Defence, Staffing, Technology.

Round 2 generated 23 items and Round 3 had 9 items that met consensus. Table 1 contains data corresponding to findings from each round of the study.

Table 1. Overall Study Findings.

Category	Round 1 Generated Statements	Round 2 Statements	Round 3 Statements	Consensus Statements	Portion of Statements Representing Consensus
Internal control	33	33	23	9	28%

Fig. 1 contains a visual representation of the first-round codes relating to internal control.

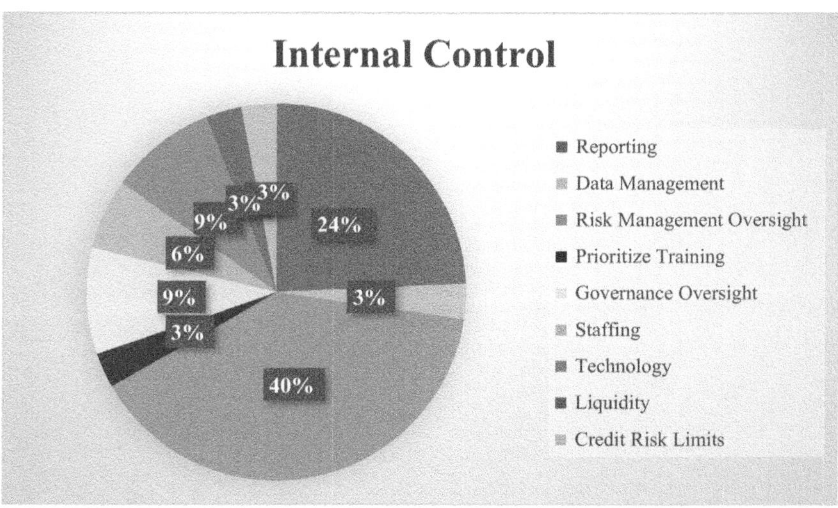

Fig. 1. First-Round Codes Related to Internal Control.

The consensus level was set to six or more out of the 10 votes. The panel of experts voting results statements were relayed to strong governance committees, reporting and escalation, established expectations for communication and reporting, ensuring employees have time to recognise problems and follow procedures and won't cut corners when they are not always under extreme pressure, automation of manual processes that are prone to human errors, monthly/quarterly reporting over controls performance to includes key performance/risk indicators, periodic risk and controls assessment, making training a priority, having a Risk Taxonomy which reflected varying degrees of desirability and feasibility which corroborates the extant literature.

Chapter 2

Significant Losses Incurred by Large Banks and SIFIs Due to Internal Control Weaknesses

Several large global companies and banks failures before, during and after the 2008 financial crises had ineffective Internal Control Systems due to poor governance and board oversight. Global banks significant losses from fraudulent actions such as: Lloyds Banking Group and Barclays in 2006 created €5.9 billion and €4 billion losses, Bernard L. Madoff Investment Securities and Société Générale in 2008 resulting in a loss of almost $17 billion and €6.3 billion, Bank of America and Citigroup in 2012 causing losses of $175.5 million and $22 million, Rabobank and Fondiaria-SAI in 2013 generating losses of $1 billion and €252 million occurred because of weak internal controls that did not prevent these fraud events from occurring (Pakhchanyan, 2016). A strong governance structure would support key controls that mitigate various risk factors that caused significant losses. The continuous unmitigated fraudulent acts, loose control environment and risk shifting are enabled by banks with weak risk management practices that contributed to the financial crisis (Lui, 2011). Risk mitigation measures should have efforts aimed at controlling fraud and surpass the minimum risk assessment set by the regulators. The importance of having strong key internal controls in place to mitigate and lower significant losses in large companies and banks was magnified after the Enron scandal and before the 2008 recession. Prior to the 2008 financial crises, the collapse of Enron was one of the first indicators of large systemically important financial institutions (SIFIs) going out of business due to weak internal control which shocked the global economy/financial sector.

Bezo and Dibra (2023) posit Enron was one of the 10 largest companies in the United States that collapsed in 2001 due to their weak control environment, failures in the checking and monitoring processes within its governance framework, and experienced significant fraudulent activities and abuse of power which went unchecked/unremediated. Enron entered a deal with one of its rival to buy the company but the rival backed out of the deal; this caused many big trading partners to discontinue conducting business with Enron which led to the company

Effective Internal Control Practices in Banks, 15–34

doi:10.1108/978-1-83662-972-620251002

collapse (Bezo & Dibra, 2023). The Board of Directors at Enron failed to do their duties in protecting the company from fraud, senior management abuse of power and mitigating risk by enforcing good governance and controls. Instead, Enron's Board of Directors waived conflict of interest rules which allowed Andrew Fastow (chief financial officer) to create private partnerships to conduct business with the firm that were deceptive in concealing debts and liabilities; this resulted in significant losses which negatively impacted Enron's reported profits (Bezo & Dibra, 2023). Enron corporate financial scandals had a global negative impact on financial markets where it undermined investors' confidence in US capital markets (Hideaki & Naoki, 2021). Al-Matari, Mohammed and Al-Matari (2017) noted corporate financial scandal had negative impacts on US markets; this led to loss of investors' confidence, less investments in the stock market, and firms had difficulties raising equity from the stock market. Enron 2001 scandal drew international attention to company failures in the United States and the root causes of these failing large organizations (Bezo & Dibra, 2023).

American International Group, Inc. (AIG) had significant losses that put the firm at risk of going out of business if they were not rescued by the government. AIG was labelled by the government as too big to fail due to its size and interconnected nature in the global economy. The losses from AIG would caused negative domino effects on the global stock market; if the company is not in receipt of rescue funds to keep it from going bankrupt, this would cause a default on payments to its' business partners. AIG executives' behaviour after receiving bailout funds caused a scandal on Wall Street. The firm took bailout funds and then paid their former chief executive a $5 million performance bonus and sent selected employees on a half-million-dollar resort trip (Robertson & Sullivan, 2009). Negative external news had a direct impact on the customer confidence in the financial markets which causes firms to suffer losses due to the investor's reaction to the news. An effective measure to maintain investors/consumer confidence is to reassure them that there is credibility in the information they rely on to make their investments. This information is usually the publicly filed financial statements of those companies, earnings news broadcasted in the media and positive news about the company in the media. There are other news that are industry and economic based that are external to the company but can have a negative direct impact on their business such as interest rates and currency devaluations. Currency devaluations (1994 Mexican peso devaluation, Russia's debt default in 1998) cause significant losses for global banks who invested heavily in Argentina (Stein, 2002).

Similarly, the banking industry which is very important to society suffered significant losses and challenges to its' internal control environment. This made the banks vulnerable to negative news and activities (Abdullah et al., 2018). The nature of the flow of money in the public sector requires effective monitoring procedures in place and regulations to retain the confidence of the public in the banking system (Abdullah et al., 2018). If there are bank runs stemming from losses to banks that ended up being insolvent, this becomes public news that eventually erodes consumer confidence. This negative news has caused consumers to panic and pulled their money out of the bank and caused investors to lower their investments. This lack of confidence in banks can erode the banking sector and spill over in both domestic and global economy. Citigroup cumulative losses in Argentina increased from US$475 million reported in 2001 fourth-quarter earnings statement to US$2.2 billion in first quarter 2002, Fleet Boston Financial Corp. had losses increased from US$1.1 billion in 2001 to US$1.3-billion in 2002, J.P. Morgan Chase & Co. losses rose from US$351- million 2001 to US$411-million 2002, and HSBC Holdings PLC reported 2002 losses in March was US$1.1 billion (Stein, 2002). The root causes of these losses need to be examined by management and design controls that will be effective in mitigating these significant systemic losses. It is necessary to have an internal control system as it is a crucial investor's tool to assess the sufficiency of corporate reporting practices; a good internal control quality (ICQ) is significantly important in achieving good financial reporting policy and credibility in the financial numbers (Al-Matari et al., 2017). Banks and significant institutions should invest in a periodic risk and controls assessment process to identify gaps, weaknesses and efficiencies in the control environment. The importance placed on having internal control processes is demonstrated in the assertion of Allen et al. (2016) that control activities enhanced through regulation requirements can contain systemic risk, reduce losses and sustain financial stability.

In Spain, Santander Central Hispano SA and Banco Bilbao Vizcaya Argentaria SA had losses of US$3.2 billion in Argentina in 2001 (Stein, 2002). Due to significant investment losses in Argentina, many banks refrain from investing funds in the country; Bank of Nova Scotia incurred a $377-million loss in 2002 an increase from $63 million loss in 2001, which caused them to stop investing in this location/country (Stein, 2002). Citigroup internal controls tied to management of excessive risk exposure in one sector and location did not prevent the bank from investing heavily in Argentina. In this region, Citigroup had US$23.6 billion of Argentine loans on their books in 2001 which exposed the bank to more losses in the subsequent months due to government's peso devaluation and debt default (Stein, 2002). Indonesia's central bank tried to conceal the magnitude of its losses from the public. Leahy (2000) states Indonesia's central bank had losses and liabilities that are billions of dollars greater than what was originally reported publicly; the actual losses incurred and liability exposure was made public through leaked documents from the external auditors, who performed an independent audit of Bank of Indonesia. The violation of internal control procedures by the Indonesia's central bank resulted in the central bank lending Rp80,248 bn (£6.7 bn) to the banking system and not appropriately accounting for Rp22,560 bn in problem foreign exchange transactions by passing proper procedures (Leahy, 2000). These failed detective and preventative controls allowed these varied banks to incur significant losses. These failed controls force banks to take a look at the risk and control framework, along their assessment process to identify poorly designed controls.

A periodic risk and controls assessment takes a snapshot of the control environment health at that point in time. Controls need to be assessed and measured periodically to ensure they meet the various regulatory guidelines such as Sarbanes–Oxley 2002, which requires a control assessment/review annually. This assessment determines if the controls are effective in meeting the regulatory laws.

Banks who do not meet regulatory laws requirements are subject to penalties, fines and losses. Additionally, the control assessment examines if the control is designed appropriately to mitigate the assigned risk. The accounting scandals of these large corporations have caused consumers to question the quality of the publicly filed financial statements numbers (Hideaki & Naoki, 2021). Customers wondered whether these firms are as profitable as they have reported. Al-Matari et al. (2017) stated these corporate scandals which occurred at Enron, Global Crossing, Tyco and World Com were linked to ineffective board and its committee's lackadaisical supervision of management; this encouraged a weak control environment which failed to prevent companies' failures. Taxpayers are tired of financing the bad behaviour of bankers on Wall Street by the Fed rescuing these banks and public companies from failures and issuance of bailout funds used to pay expensive bonuses to rich bankers (Fahey, 2016). Financial wealth and monies were transferred from middle-class Americans to very wealthy bankers which encourages more irresponsible behaviour (Fahey, 2016). Many have requested sound regulatory reforms that addresses socially unacceptable mechanism that let banks privatise their profits and ask the public for help when there is a risk hurricane that became unstoppable (Petitjean, 2013). The passing of Dodd–Frank Bill, 2010, and the issuance of Basel III regulations were efforts from domestic and global governments to curtail high-risk behaviour in banks that caused significant losses.

Basel III liquidity regulations were seen as a possible solution to bank insolvency by Gastón and Schumacher (2017) who assert the regulation could decrease the probabilities of default for banks. The default risk of banks during a crisis episode could have been mitigated if Basel III was launched; there would be improvements to the financial soundness of the banking sector (Gastón & Schumacher, 2017). It was noted by Boora and Kavita (2018) that Basel-III norms intention was to increase the resiliency of banks through effective risk management practices. As noted by Herring (2016), banks must but also demonstrate to regulators that they will be able to remain in compliance to capital ratio requirements. The internal control monitoring activities of the regulators include intervention with banks that fall below minimum capital requirement (Abou-El-Sood, 2017). Banks have received recommendations from compliance and assurance guidance that they should develop effective strategies and policies to comply with capital adequacy requirements (Boora & Kavita, 2018). Banks have to treat the requirements with expediency as this regulation is mandatory for banks to become Basel-compliant (Boora & Kavita, 2018). Banks rolled out an enterprise-level risk management tool developed in house which took years before they can go live; as a result, banks resolved to the employment of a third-party risk assessment and modelling tool to assist with compliance and documented risk appetite (Lee, 2015). Banks should consider linking their developed risk appetite, stress-testing processes, capital plans to capture the full range of material exposures and employ multiple conceptually sound activities and approaches (Lee, 2015). Banks in their development of their internal control framework focus on the development and monitoring of models should take into consideration segregation of duties for the process owners/teams involved in the process. Model validation teams' duties and responsibilities, review and approvals, should be different from model risk managers (Goldberg, 2017). The responsibilities of model risk management teams entail the development and use of sound models, governance, control mechanisms such as board and senior management oversight, policies/procedures, controls and compliance (Goldberg, 2017). Model risk managers in their efforts to understand the nature and magnitude of embedded risk spend a significant amount of time talking with the risk takers (Goldberg, 2017). This is essential in the design and operation of models that should accurately project capital levels as low levels that don't meet requirements and caused them to receive penalties from regulators (Abou-El-Sood, 2017). Additionally, banks can be placed into receivership if they are significantly under-capitalised (Abou-El-Sood, 2017).

Governments and central banks' handouts during a crisis have created the biggest moral hazard (Petitjean, 2013). The focus on ethics, strong morals and integrity have been highlighted as lacking in the banking sector which Tourigny et al. (2003) noted as a gap in exhibited behaviour reflecting principles of governance and ethical standards tied to bank failures. Noreen et al. (2016) assert regulatory authorities' focus should be directed at ways to control the moral hazard behaviour of banks. Lui (2011) pointed out that bank managers' lack of morals and ethics caused them to seek their self-interest in gains at the expense of exposing shareholders to significant losses from their investments in high-risk products. To understand the root cause of bank managers' self-interest, an examination has to take place of what motivated them to invest in high-risk products with upfront significant shorter gains that generate significant losses in the long run, which revealed the motive is embedded in agency and goal theory. The role of incentives as per Chawla (2016) provides a theoretical understanding of the root cause of the problem between shareholder and manager. The aims of shareholder and manager are not harmonised which caused conflicting interest and objectives between the two parties which is tied to risky behaviours of agents (Darayseh & Chazi, 2018). Principal-Agency theory and Goal theory as noted by Lui (2011) addresses root causes of reckless behaviour of bank managers/agents; these agents pursued their own financial interest and exposed shareholder/principal to high risk in investments and losses. Similarly, Darayseh and Chazi (2018) assert principal–agent theory identified the problem between shareholder and manager. Bank agents do not operate in the best interest of the principal/shareholder because of conflicting interest and objectives between both parties (Darayseh & Chazi, 2018).

Chawla (2016) noted goal theory highlights the role of incentives and motives carried out through the use of commission plans which motivate individuals to reach target goal. Similarly, Sepdiningtyas and Santoso (2017) contend goal theory use incentives to motivate bankers and garner their commitments to these goals. The examination of the concepts of intrinsic and extrinsic motivations revealed contractual incentives tied to unclear goals, created by principals to motivate agents to meet sales targets, which led them to display dysfunctional behavioural (Osterloh & Frey, 2000). Banks cannot ignore a significant issue that arises in principal–agent theory which caused tensions in the relationship; the agent seeks to maximise personal wealth while forgoing their role in meeting principal personal interest of wealth maximisation (Darayseh & Chazi, 2018). This disagreement in principal and agent objectives established in the relationship leads to behavioural conflicts (Darayseh & Chazi, 2018). This type of agents' risky behaviour arose in the 2008 financial crisis. This financial crisis was partly caused by weaknesses that created multiple principal/agent problems, information asymmetry, adverse selection, moral hazard, mortgage fraud, predatory lending, model errors, managerial slack, unidentified risk, laxed internal control environment (Lui, 2011). Principal–agent problems caused a misalignment of party's incentives, excessive leverage and risk-taking lined to financial crisis and the issuance of bad loans due to a weak risk management environment (Lui, 2011). Agents can increase their personal income while decreasing their efforts due to different working motivations in the principal and agent relationship (Darayseh & Chazi, 2018). Commission plans have been used extensively in banks to motivate individual to reach target goal (Chawla, 2016). Sepdiningtyas and Santoso (2017) asserts incentives are key factors in motivating bankers to commit to company sales goals. Many organizations motivate their salespeople using rewards and punishments; this can backfire and lead to be disengaged salesperson and poor organizational reputation (Chawla, 2016).

The concepts of intrinsic and extrinsic motivations underscored the importance of having clearly defined goals to garner positive results; the opposite of this reveals that duplicitous, unclear contractual incentives tied to goals established by principals to motivate agents can cause dysfunctional behaviour (Osterloh & Frey, 2000). Employees are extrinsically motivated through monetary compensation that gives immediate gratification (Osterloh & Frey, 2000). This type of instant gratification gives satisfaction to the individual independent of the actual activity; this knowledge is exploited by firms who link this extrinsically motivated monetary incentive to the goals of the bank (Osterloh & Frey, 2000). Banks that practice strict pay-for-performance incentive system without contraining rules experience employees display of opportunistic and self-interest behaviour (Osterloh & Frey, 2000). Bank's employees display this behaviour evident in the subprime bubble of 2003–07 exploited by senior managers (Calomiris, 2009). Bank's senior managers established compensation systems that reward subordinates on sales, total assets managed, total revenues collected; subordinates took additional risk to meet these goals and expand portfolios without any regard to risk, future potential loss (Calomiris, 2009). Senior managers benefited from this high-risk behaviour exhibited by employees when they attained these goals by rewarding themselves with large short-term bonuses from the profits (Calomiris, 2009). Senior managers collected significant bonuses upfront on high risk investments as there are no restrictions or wait periods in place for payouts earned on risky investments; they cash out their stock options prior to the company suffering losses (Calomiris, 2009).

Another factor goal theory revealed is the employees need rewards and promotions from their supervisors to improve their performance (Sepdiningtyas & Santoso, 2017). Motel (2016) highlights strong and negative behaviours stemming from the intense cognitive focus on achieving established goals (Motel, 2016). There need to be some degree of goal acceptance and commitment to reach assigned goals and contribute to positive employee performance; this level of commitment to these goals would help the employee to strive to meet these expectations (Motel, 2016). A bank employee who was highly motivated by intrinsic self interest caused JP Morgan Chase bank to incur US$6 billion in losses referred to as the London Whale scandal in 2012 (Ertürk, 2016; Handorf, 2017). Qualitative methods are used to examine the application of goal theory to senior manager's behaviour in bank holding company setting which provides an understanding of the reward systems; this highlights how these systems in bank incentivize risky senior bank manager's activities and investments (Ertürk, 2016). Intense market competition can be a motivational factor that caused senior bank managers in their effort to achieve their goals (in this, competitive markets take on excessive risk [Mcmillan & Mcmillan, 2016]).

Large banks who have a sizeable market share concentration and have low profits are motivated to consider a mergers; this oftentimes do not add value added and can increase the levels of bank risk reflected in their Z-score and equity capital (Mcmillan & Mcmillan, 2016). There were some elements of dysfunction behaviour influenced by senior managers goals exhibited in MF Global bankruptcy filing in 2011 (Mcmillan & Mcmillan, 2016). MF Global investments in the European debt crisis caused them to incur losses more than $1.5 billion through overly aggressive trading strategies (Mcmillan & Mcmillan, 2016). Banks are intrinsically and extrinsically motivated by federal government bailout programs, and protection from the Fed during times of crisis; this encouraged banks senior managers to engage in more high-risk activities (Dandapani et al., 2017). The Fed thought the bailout of institutions with public money was a necessary mitigation measure they had to take to prevent negative consequences of their failure (Pollick et al., 2016). This established a global standard around the world that bailouts of large banks by the government are necessary to prevent bank runs (Pollick et al., 2016). Global governments saw rescuing failing banks with public funds may be a viable systemic solution that could prevent risk of loss and disruption of credit and payment services to customers (Pollick et al., 2016). Government intervention and bailouts have incentivised banks into higher risk-taking by their bank subsidiary (Dandapani et al., 2017). Another dysfunctional behaviour displayed by senior bank manager is their use of shadow banks caused by the additional capital demands by Basel III (Deos et al., 2015).

The demands of raising and maintaining capital levels established by the regulators induced bankers to go back into shadow-banking activities; this was managers' plot to generate more profits or lower-cost operations (Deos et al., 2015). The increase in shadow-banking activities increased risk-taking levels at a reduced margin, adversely impacting bank's stability (Lin et al., 2018). Banks became financially disturbed when shadow-banking activities over run into normal banking activities and negatively impact the economy (Lin et al., 2018). These negative visible impacts were overlooked by senior bank managers who continued to engage in multiple shadow-banking activities such as wealth management products (WMPs), entrusted loans (ELs) (Lin et al., 2018). This increase in shadow-banking activities leads to a transfer of wealth from equity holders to the debt holders and increases insurance liabilities (Lin et al., 2018). Bank managers' short-term returns mindset was a moral hazard to future and profitability of the bank; these employees over ride the bank's charter value which they are sworn to uphold as agents (Noreen et al., 2016). Managers seek earning short run profits and ignore the future sustainability of the firm, which is a form of principal and agent problem (Noreen et al., 2016). The motivation of employees through the use of equity incentives causes managers to go overboard, to take risks at the expense of creditors (Tung, 2011). This gamblers' mentality exhibited by managers can be mitigated by rolling out a new approach to compensation; this entails managers paid in part with their banks' public subordinated debt securities (Tung, 2011).

Banking regulatory authorities must strive to control this moral hazard behaviour in bank managers by putting in place restrictions and parameters on how banks go about meeting their capital adequacy ratio (Noreen et al., 2016). Dowd and Hutchinson (2016) argue large banks being under-capitalised is a continuous issue that needs to be mitigated, which is partly to be blamed on regulators propping them up when they have increased losses. Some banks that operate in an effective control environment have increased their focus on maintaining sound capital adequacy; this is aligned to risk-based capital standards (Kaur & Kapoor, 2015). Subsequent to the passing of the Dodd–Frank Bill, 2010, there are some banks that continue to be distressed and require close regulatory supervision (Kolari & Ivan, 2017). The Fed keeping an eye on chronically stressed institutions may return systemic risk to normal levels (Kolari & Ivan, 2017). The aims of Basel III capital adequacy standards and Dodd–Frank Bill, 2010, are to improve capital adequacy through performance of controls around stress tests and supervisory oversight of safety and soundness measures (Kolari & Ivan, 2017). The Fed conducted independent stress test of large banks which identified several banks had insufficient capital; Bank of America had to raise additional capital, Morgan Stanley was required to revise capital, Deutsche and Santander prohibited from paying dividends and stock buybacks (Walker et al., 2017). The efforts of the Fed to solve the problem of banks facing insolvency by implementing enhanced risk management measures, stronger reliance on capital, continuously fall short of its goals (Handorf, 2017). A robust risk mitigation plan should consider model risk measures and identify economically dangerous uncertainties, risk factors, data quality, estimating probabilities that quantify risk (Baker et al., 2015). The Fed should require bank managers to take into consideration quantitative assessment and risk measurement approach that incorporate embedded risk in financial decision-making (Baker et al., 2015). Additionally, there are factors linked to risk drivers in the investment portfolio, and management activities that should be considered in the design of risk mitigation activities (Baker et al., 2015). Risk management framework should encompass three major components of risk analysis (modelling, measuring, managing) that will create a framework that will enable a firm to cope with risk during extreme events (Baker et al., 2015).

The magnitude of losses due to lax controls and governance motivated congress to roll out a multiagency system approach to financial regulation (Fischer, 2015). Both the reckless behaviour of bank managers and the complex designed of the products caused the regulators to impose risk-based capital requirements like Basel Norms (Kaur & Kapoor, 2015). The complexities in the banking industry contributed to systemic growth of losses Congress tried to mitigate. Congress designed a regulatory framework utilising multiple overlapping agencies namely; Commodity Futures Trading Commission (CFTC), self-regulatory organizations (SROs), Chicago Mercantile Exchange, and National Futures Association (NFA) used to monitor derivatives in banks and public companies (Fischer, 2015). CFTC is tasked with regulation of the implementation and management of risk linked to derivative transactions, oversight supervisors for derivative transactions, setting capital limits and punishment of members who violate the established regulatory rules (Fischer, 2015). Capital regulation requirements require actionable activities from management defined in their policies and procedures, risk control matrix and internal risk monitoring framework that ensures they meet government guidelines.

Banks have to ensure internal controls in place assist them to timely meet Dodd–Frank Act 2010 laws, which requires large banks providing loan-level data on their commercial real estate loan portfolios support for Comprehensive Capital Analysis and Review (CCAR) (Black et al., 2017). This loan data that support the CCAR filing enable regulators to perform analysis of the portfolio loans from origination to renegotiation (Black et al., 2017). Internal control processes are imperative to have in place as noted by Allen et al. (2016) that control activities received an enhancement from the new capital regulations requirements of Dodd–Frank Wall Street Reform and Consumer Protection Act (DFA), 2010; the aim of DFA, 2010, is to contain systemic risk and maintaining financial stability. DFA of 2010 objectives are rooted in its efforts to ban most proprietary trading in banks with federally insured deposits (Trendowski & Rustambekov, 2017). Proprietary trading speculation, hedge or private equity funds should be bifurcated from FDIC-insured entity and acting as a depository institution (Johnson, 2015). Banks should not be profit trading at risk of the public (Johnson, 2015). There are some exemptions if the trades are related to market-making and meet at least seven standards highlighted by the regulators (Trendowski & Rustambekov, 2017). Banks are required to submit Dodd–Frank Asset Stress Tests (DFAST) to regulators to prove they meet the capital ratio requirements (Herring, 2016). Banks need to be able to demonstrate they have sufficient capital to cover loan losses, survive and stay afloat of financial shocks during recessions (Petersen et al., 2009). The idiosyncratic banking risk requires bank manager to exercise market discipline that is both credible and effective (Petersen et al., 2009).

Banks should maintain debts that could convert to capital in response to specific market indicators, financial distress and help mitigate the possibility of their failures (Allen et al., 2016). Managers would be deterred from taking on risks that might lead to bank failures which could dilute existing shareholders (Allen et al., 2016). Another pressing problem is the lack of regulatory reform to address the weaknesses stemming from housing finance system; there has been no real reform in response to the mortgage crisis (Allen et al., 2016). The stress test requirements rolled out by Dodd–Frank Bill, 2010, required the use of models. The Monte-Carlo simulation is an activity used for generating VaR-figures across different desks, aggregating risks used in stress test calculations (Bellof & Wehn, 2018). Dynamic Stochastic General Equilibrium (DSGE) is another model used to investigate the relationship between bank capital adequacy and the boom-bust cycle in the recent financial crisis (Fukuda, 2016). There is difficulty in models to analyse and project the relationship between the financial conditions of financial intermediaries and the business cycle (Fukuda, 2016). Additionally, the models had errors in the analysis of the relationships between fluctuation in prices and entrepreneurs' debt after financial contracts are taken into consideration (Fukuda, 2016). DSGE analyses various shocks (monetary shock, capital price shock with no news shock, capital price shock with a news shocks) which revealed a positive monetary shock decreases output; a capital price shock with no news shock is simply a positive capital price shock that increases loan volumes (Fukuda, 2016).

The performance of stress test is a mundane task which requires significant amount of human and monetary resources, calculation stress scenario using multitude of quantitative models (Denev & Mutnikas, 2016). The success of performing these stress test faced hindrances from internal organizational silos, bureaucracy and legacy software systems (Denev & Mutnikas, 2016). Stress test is a useful compliance activity, complex in nature, onerous activity that pulls bank executives away from mission-critical business objectives (Lee, 2015). Bank managers' focus pivoted to months of data compilation and ongoing meetings with regulators (Lee, 2015). There is the reliance nature of these stress testing activities that is being questioned as a result of inaccuracy of these stress test measures (Baradaran, 2014). Many individuals questioned whether they pose significant danger to the financial sector stability because of inability to predict actual market risk and losses (Baradaran, 2014). These models run based on reliance on historical data and events and the test of static balance sheet which can be a weakness (Baradaran, 2014). Fed capital compliance demands, burdens and cost incurred from running these stress test models have been a concern that these can hamper banks maintaining profitability or international competitive advantages (Fahey, 2016). Glasserman and Tangirala (2016) state Fed requires banks to invest in resource, control structure to ensure they meet the new requirements and perform risk-assessment to prove their financially stable. The other challenges posed by human errors incurred during the implementation or use of models, operational risk, model risk caused by conscious selection of assumptions that has embedded risk (Bellof & Wehn, 2018). These risk models require valuation models to perform a test/validation prior to roll out of the actual model to demonstrate that a certain dependency exists (Bellof & Wehn, 2018).

The models used in the Fed stress test lack transparency in the stress testing scenarios (Bellof & Wehn, 2018). Employees performing the stress test need for further improvement in the information for them to accurately understand running the Fed models (Crabb, 2018). There are risks embedded in models that need exploration to gain understanding in areas such as: estimation errors, parameter uncertainties caused by algorithmic methods use of statistics, computational estimators used in the model framework, individual model assumptions, variations used in the algorithm and challenger models replaced by alternative model algorithm assumptions (Bellof & Wehn, 2018). There are risks from credit projections, models used in studies being wrong from interconnections within the model ecosystem (Goldberg, 2017). Bankers need to understand the dynamics of models which have inputs, assumptions, calculations, quantitative outputs, developer thought at point in time and the overall intended set of uses (Goldberg, 2017). There are ecosystem's risks linked to market data and databases, computer and nonautomated systems, assumptions and calculations, business decisions, developers, humans and computer programs, model validations past and present and policies (Goldberg, 2017). The use of stress tests models should be assessed for uncertainties of the model due to estimation errors, local variations of the model components, use of challenger models that can make them useful in decisions, business-specific statements and avoid redundant assessments; a clear distinction must be made for operational risk (Belloff & Wehn, 2018). Stress tests must be rigorous in scope of coverage and scenario design so that the results are convincing; the actual health of banks, the timing of the exercise, market conditions and public receptiveness to the disclosures are essential to a successful stress test (Ong & Pazarbasioglu, 2014).

Idiosyncratic risk that is systemic in nature should be taken into consideration when designing internal controls. Idiosyncratic risks spread through interconnected banks, financial networks that transfer losses and gains alike through the network. Interconnected networks make transfer among banks to facilitate stability and absorb any negative idiosyncratic shocks (Allen et al., 2016). The drawback to interconnected structure is its potential to easily cause instability which makes banks in this network vulnerable; large losses can be transmitted to other banks and expose the entire financial system to systemic failures (Allen et al., 2016). SIFI banks function as interconnected multinational banks such as the 10 biggest banks in the United States whose capital-to-asset ratios fell to less than 3% which send alarming signals to regulators (Dowd & Hutchinson, 2016). SIFI banks with low capital levels with the possibility of incurring significant losses is a going concern for the government as this is a sign banks can become insolvent. Government authorities (Federal Reserve Bank, Federal Deposit Insurance Corporate, Federal Government) provided bailout funds to these large banks due to their size, reach, systemic nature to prevent their failures which pose a systemic risk to the economy (Dowd & Hutchinson, 2016). Wan (2016) had reservations about interconnected financial system and their role in spreading weaknesses among banks evidenced in global financial crisis of 2008. There are other SIFIs that are insurance companies that play important roles in the banking and the financial system. The role of these SIFIs such as AIG posed a systemic risk which needs to be regulated.

Banks continue to be under-capitalised as noted by Dowd and Hutchinson (2016) by their engagement in excessive risk products with the reliance on regulators to prop them up. On the other hand, some banks have increased their focus on maintaining sound capital adequacy and adhered to the risk-based capital standards (Kaur & Kapoor, 2015). This was evident subsequent to crisis period 2010–2012 where some banks continued to be distressed and require regulatory supervision (Kolari & Ivan, 2017). These chronically stressed institutions need regulatory intervention to implement monitoring and detective controls to enhance their priorities of helping these banks return systemic risk levels to normal levels (Kolari & Ivan, 2017). The main objectives of the Basel capital adequacy standards are driven towards strengthening stress tests and effectively provide supervisory oversight of safety and soundness (Kolari & Ivan, 2017). Congress has integrated governance, risk management and macro-prudential regulatory measures enforce supervision and regulation with more robust laws for winding up or resolving too big to fail financial institutions (Guynn, 2010). Banks have to adhere to stronger requirements as noted in greater counter-cyclical capital, liquidity, maximum leverage requirements, regulation of executive compensation and over-the-counter derivatives regulation (Guynn, 2010). The execution of the regulatory rules by the designated authorities had failures caused by the complexity of the regulatory constellation and daunting intellectual demands (Viljanen, 2016). The regulators had a gap in their understanding of existing bank's business processes incorrect identification and modification techniques, which caused weak impacts and changes (Viljanen, 2016). In order for the regulators to devise effective implementation strategies to obtain success, they should seek to understand the entire bank's business process that will result in the desired behavioural change (Viljanen, 2016). The use of the Basel Accords to mitigate capital risk was ineffective; this was partly because of the heavy focus on risk weights, risk models captured by the banking industry which failed to reduce risk and losses (Dowd & Hutchinson, 2016). There are challenges in the execution of identified regulation to mitigate weak internal control lies in the internal effective implementation strategies.

CFTC struggles to strike a balance between public regulation and self-regulation while monitoring banks and public companies compliance with policy (Fischer, 2015). CFTC allowed banks to experience cost savings through the benefits of cost internalisation where SROs perform their review of the rules and file the results with the CFTC (Fischer, 2015). CFTC have experience their own internal challenges that will require them to conduct self-assessment to improve use of its resources; this will inevitably improve their oversight functions of banks and public companies (Fischer, 2015). However, information asymmetry weaknesses affect all stakeholders of the information including internal management, investors and the regulators that rely on this information to carry out their task and mandates. The lack of information asymmetry among bank stakeholders contributed to significant losses (Abou-El-Sood, 2017). The lack of information asymmetry became a hindrance to fulfilment of the demands for non-financial reporting disclosure used to make social performance decisions (Stubbs & Higgins, 2018). There is a lack of timely and clearly documented information due to lack of effective controls around corporate reporting and meeting the needs of the investment community (Stubbs & Higgins, 2018). The corporate reports is confusing, cluttered, fragmented, disconnected, wordy, complex and compliance driven which made its usefulness questionable when making financial and risk-driven decisions (Stubbs & Higgins, 2018).

The timely access to data, completeness and accuracy of the information have been a challenge to the regulators. Regulatory data quality and accessibility has been a concern for regulators caused by the data storage on separate information systems, and teams had no accessibility to the information where it is stored (Alampalli, 2013). This prevents the various overlapping agencies designated by Congress to regulate bank risk and practice the routine sharing of information between the regulators (Alampalli, 2013). The gaps data access and sharing posed to managing banks risk should be address; this will aid the systemic regulatory framework to function as intended by the government (Alampalli, 2013). The world looks to mitigation measures that are possible through strong corporate governance in failure prevention; the scope of corporate governance encompasses a country's (private and public, formal and informal) institutions who work in concert to govern the relationship between the people who manage corporations (corporate insiders) and various investors' resources in corporations around the world (Bezo & Dibra, 2023). The Government has used monetary policy measures to address bank risk in their governance role and international bank regulatory strategy to reduce broad money growth to curtail financial crisis (Hanke & Sekerke, 2017). The Federal Reserve offsets the monetary effects of these enhanced regulatory policies through quantitative easing (QE) (Hanke & Sekerke, 2017). This has delayed and diverted attention from obstacles to money creation in the banking system and ease public tensions (Hanke & Sekerke, 2017). In concert with these efforts, the Fed put in place requirements that banks are required to show how their balance sheet holds up in a hypothetically adverse and severely adverse scenario (Hanke & Sekerke, 2017).

Fed provides extreme assumptions to be used as part of the analysis used by management such as the stock market crashes, skyrocketing unemployment, which should be used in CCAR submissions which run up to 10,000 pages (Fahey, 2016). Banks are required to develop their macroeconomic scenarios using a statistical model Vector Autoregression (VAR) to employ dependency structure between both macroeconomic drivers and modelling segments (Jacobs, 2016). Independent calculations are performed by the Fed to compute capital projections under each scenario and compared to the bank's capital projections (Gorton, 2015). Capital gaps discovered by the Fed in their independent calculations are examined and if considered, significant would require shortfalls filled by Fed through the Capital Assistance Program (CAP) (Gorton, 2015). Fed had backstop which functions as a bridge for banks to access private capital for the capital gaps through the Treasury's CAP and stress tests (Gorton, 2015). This was an attempt by the Fed to prepare banks in the wake of a large negative shock to the system they would be alerted and take measure to recapitalised following an adverse shock and raise new capital (Greenwood et al., 2017). Banks that practise good governance had adequate information in a timely manner, larger capital ratios and undertake less risky positions (Abou-El-Sood, 2017). There are some governance controls that the panel of experts voted on that they deemed to be ineffective and inefficient in preventing fraud due to their limitations and the possibility of overrides. Some initial second round voting on governance statements that had low desirability and feasibility ratings from the panel of experts are noted below. These statements Round 2 votes are displayed in Tables (2–4) (Velez, 2020).

Table 2. Governance Practices on Basel Principles 2nd Round Data: Non-Consensus.

Statement	Ratings	Total Number of Panelist Who Selected Each Ratings
Statement 12 – Governance practices senior bank managers can implement towards capital regulation that are effective in reducing losses entails adherence to the Basel principles around managing risk.		
	Highly undesirable: Will have major negative effect.	1
	Undesirable: Will have a negative effect with little or no positive effect.	0
	Neither desirable nor undesirable: Will have equal positive and negative effects.	3
	Desirable: Will have a positive effect with minimum negative effects.	2
	Highly desirable: Will have a positive effect and little or no negative effect.	1
	Definitely infeasible: Cannot be implemented (unworkable).	0
	Probably infeasible: Some indication this cannot be implemented.	0
	May or may not be feasible: Contradictory evidence this can be implemented.	2

Table 2. *(Continued)*

Statement	Ratings	Total Number of Panelist Who Selected Each Ratings
	Probably feasible: Some indication this can be implemented.	5
	Definitely feasible: Can be implemented.	5

Table 3. Governance Practices Self-Regulation Credit Trading 2nd Round Data: Non-Consensus.

Statement	Ratings	Total Number of Panelist Who Selected Each Ratings
Statement 17 – Governance practices senior bank managers can implement towards capital regulation that are effective in reducing losses entails risk management and controls, self-regulation not to be over exposed in any area i.e. credit trading.		
	Highly undesirable: Will have major negative effect.	1
	Undesirable: Will have a negative effect with little or no positive effect.	1
	Neither desirable nor undesirable: Will have equal positive and negative effects.	1
	Desirable: Will have a positive effect with minimum negative effects.	2

(Continued)

Table 3. *(Continued)*

Statement	Ratings	Total Number of Panelist Who Selected Each Ratings
	Highly desirable: Will have a positive effect and little or no negative effect.	2
	Definitely infeasible: Cannot be implemented (unworkable).	0
	Probably infeasible: Some indication this cannot be implemented.	2
	Probably feasible: Some indication this can be implemented.	5
	Definitely feasible: Can be implemented.	3

Table 4. Governance Practices Adherence to Diversification 2nd Round Data: Non-Consensus.

Statement	Ratings	Total Number of Panelist Who Selected Each Ratings
Statement 18 – Governance practices senior bank managers can implement towards capital regulation that are effective in reducing losses entails adherence to diversification.		
	Highly undesirable: Will have major negative effect.	2
	Undesirable: Will have a negative effect with little or no positive effect.	0

Table 4. *(Continued)*

Statement	Ratings	Total Number of Panelist Who Selected Each Ratings
	Neither desirable nor undesirable: Will have equal positive and negative effects.	2
	Desirable: Will have a positive effect with minimum negative effects.	2
	Highly desirable: Will have a positive effect and little or no negative effect.	2
	Definitely infeasible: Cannot be implemented (unworkable).	0
	Probably infeasible: Some indication this cannot be implemented.	0
	May or may not be feasible: Contradictory evidence this can be implemented.	2
	Probably feasible: Some indication this can be implemented.	4
	Definitely feasible: Can be implemented.	5

Additionally, there are significant losses that banks subsidiaries incurred which have to be absorbed by the parent company which exasperated the parent company losses. For Example, Bank of Montreal incurred in 2001 credit losses of more than $500 million of which $200 million of the losses were related to bad loan provisions relating to Chicago-based Harris Bank a subsidiary of the Bank of Montreal; these significant losses incurred by bank outweighs the bank net income that year of only $4 million (Shannon, 2001). The continuous reporting of significant losses by banks had consumers/investors questioning the root causes of these losses and the transparency of the banks. Canniffe (2002) posits banks parent company started to investigate the losses that occurred in the subsidiaries such as AIB's investigation of its All first subsidiary $750 million (EUR864 million) foreign exchange loss which was deemed to be collusion within the bank and/or by external parties such as its alleged rogue trader, Mr Rusnak. The key controls of All first came into question in specific was the controls designed to stipulate who the acceptable deal counterparties were, are these controls overridden, why were the failures of the controls not detected by the compliance staff at All first (Canniffe, 2002). The failures to prevent rogue trading at All first brought key controls existence and design into question. The specific questions to the existence and functioning of these key controls related to why were significant losses of $3 million per trading day conducted by an ordinary trader without being detected (Canniffe, 2002). There are questions around triggering the All first alarm bells which are controls that operated as key risk indicators that would have alerted the bank to the trade violations in a timely manner. For example, key risk indicators that monitor trader's limits, contract confirmations that would indicate potential problems with red alerting to issue, yellow approaching being a potential issue and green means operating within guidelines and not an issue. Canniffe (2002) mentioned there were questions such as was trader operating outside his daily and overnight deal limits, was there awareness of this act by someone else in the division and they helped the perpetrator conceal this act, did he receive extra time assistance to cover up these significant trade losses? There were also questions around internal controls not being effective due to how they were performed by management such as were the daily and overnight limits properly monitored, who was the process owner that was reconciling contract confirmations against details of the deals supplied by the trader, which process owner performed the documentation review and was there appropriate segregation of duties in performing these control activities? (Canniffe, 2002). The lack of appropriate segregation of duties was tied to the root cause of trader collusion in the fraudulent trade activities, internal administration staff and external parties and individuals who provided fake documentation that turned out to be bogus options contracts (Canniffe, 2002). These fraudulent trade activities manifested in HSBC England bank.

Britain has its share of banking scandals which had caused significant losses. HSBC England's largest bank apologised to the US Senate during the summer of 2012 for the role it played in facilitating a multibillion-dollar money laundering operation for the illegal drugs trade (Cowie, 2012). This was not the first fraudulent trading scandal in Britain. Barings Bank in Britain experiences significant losses of $1.4 billion from a rogue trader in Singapore which caused the bank to become insolvent (Gullo & Kalish, 1995). The lack of effective internal control was the root cause of Baring Bank demise which allowed a trader to be in charge both of trading and the backroom operations that monitor trades which was a lack of segregation of duties, monitoring activities ad he was policing himself (Gullo & Kalish, 1995). Similarly, Eldridge and Lynch (1995) stated Barings Bank demise was cause by a trader who single handedly caused the bank to experience $790 million in losses on Asian derivatives trades. The bank was unable to cover the trade that resulted in the bank incurring significant losses which Britain central bank stepped in and shut down the bank (Eldridge & Lynch, 1995).

Japan had its share of fraud and trading scandals. Gullo and Kalish (1995) posit one of Daiwa Bank of Japan bond trader committed one of history's largest trading fraud in the New York Branch resulted in $1.1 billion US in losses which he tried to conceal with bank's records. The magnitude and length of time which spanned several years these losses was a result of 30,000 unauthorized trades executed over 11 years which went undetected for significant period of time (Gullo & Kalish, 1995). This is a clear violation of the internal controls that would have been established for the bank to operate and function/conduct its business. Several banks have been battered by a series of shocks linked to them being implicated in mis-sale of payment protection insurance and fraudulent manipulation of the London Interbank Offered Rate (Libor) causing billions of pounds in losses and being named in litigation in the United States (Cowie, 2012). England's Lloyd bank had to set aside 4.3 bn pounds to pay compensation to customers it fraudulently sold policies (Cowie, 2012). Newlands and Makortoff (2018) assert Barclays experienced losses in Q1 2018 relating to payment protection insurance (PPI) charges and a £1.4 billion settlement with the US Department of Justice (DoJ); the bank's had pre-taxed loss of £236 million Q1 2018, $2 bn (£1.4 bn) settlement with the US DOJ related to the sale of mortgage-backed securities shortly before the 2008 financial crisis. In the United States, the government played a role in the mortgage crisis through its' Government-sponsored enterprises (GSEs), Fannie Mae and Freddie Mac vehicle, which allowed individual homebuyers to afford a home by purchasing these mortgages from banks and financial intermediaries (Mamonov & Benbunan-Fich, 2017).

Many of these individuals would not have been qualified for a mortgage without the GSE, and this government involvement created a liquidity in the mortgage markets (Mamonov & Benbunan-Fich, 2017). This made it easier for individual homebuyers to acquire financing and as time went on individuals began defaulting on their loans (Mamonov & Benbunan-Fich, 2017). GSEs had loose underwriting standards prior to the 2008 financial crisis, after which Fannie Mae's made efforts to mitigate growing and delinquencies by tightening mortgage qualifications which was too late (Mamonov & Benbunan-Fich, 2017). The various components and dynamics that are a part of the elasticity of the housing supply should be monitored as they have embedded risk factors (Malpezzi, 2017). This means that land use and development regulations should be connected to real measured externalities which help lower detection risk and give regulators sense when the market is in trouble from an early onset (Malpezzi, 2017). Regulators domestic and international should invest in the timely sharing of information as this will booster effective monitoring of the housing and financial markets and transparency (Malpezzi, 2017). Mortgage-backed securities embedded risk was underrated as many banks as possible who invested in these products were unaware of the high risk of potential losses in these products.

Crawford (2017) mentioned mortgage-backed securities were high-risk products that were not appropriately monitored, and they were rated as AAA was not reflective of default and interest rate risks of the mortgage loans. Additionally, Barclay's banks reserved in 2018 an extra £400m to cover PPI charges to address the significant number of complaints (Newlands & Makortoff, 2018). Local and International government seek to carry out measures and interferences to restore investor confidence as seen in many of the large banks being rescued from insolvency.

Chapter 3

Global Economic Impact Due to Weak Controls in Banking and Financial Services

The US bank failures negatively impacted the global banking sector which resulted in the federal government providing billions of dollars to failing banks to prop them up and prevent bank runs (Aksoy & Mohammed, 2020). Banks failures were tied to poor leadership who failed to practise sound and effective internal controls. Barr (2017) asserts there was a lack of accountability at the top of the bank which negatively impacted the control environment. This made the control environment susceptible to high risk from its exposure to abusive high-frequency trading practices (Barr, 2017). High-risk trades increased investor losses and fees that went unchecked because of conflicts of interest by top leaders (Barr, 2017). This weak control environment lack effective activities to prevent high risk behaviour in managers; Osterloh and Frey (2000) noted the banks had pay for performance incentives, no behaviour constrained, and rules were not used to restrict high risk activities. Many manages were motivated by self-interest that were pursued with guile with no restrain from rules and regulations (Osterloh & Frey, 2000). Bank leaders' activities were motivated by shorter profits, large bonuses and self-rewards (Lui, 2011; Sepdiningtyas & Santoso, 2017). These managers' negative behaviours were linked to intense cognitive and behavioural focus that caused them to vigorously purse established goals achievement at significant cost (Motel, 2016). Both managers and subordinates accepted and were committed to these goals with overwhelming pursuits (Motel, 2016). There were no internal control constraints to ensure the high risk activities that generated large profits were in adherence to key controls; this would mitigate the risk of significant losses. Instead, leaders' bad actions were passed to their subordinates who often times replicate the same behaviour.

Leaders incentivized their subordinates to increase sales and portfolios in high-risk products which resulted in significant losses (Lui, 2011; Sepdiningtyas & Santoso, 2017). This was evident in the compensation system established by bank leaders who rewarded their subordinates when they were able to achieve the high sales targets set for them (Aiyar et al., 2015). Additionally, revenue targets set at a benchmark was used as one of the metrics in the compensation system which caused subordinates to expand their portfolio of trades and various high-risk

Effective Internal Control Practices in Banks, 35–47

doi:10.1108/978-1-83662-972-620251003

products to meet these objectives set by their supervisors (Aiyar et al., 2015). There was no regard for the nature of the high risk and potential significant losses. The subordinates were focused on the large short-term bonuses their managers dangled in front of them to push them across the finish line of meeting the compensation system's unhealthy goals. Aiyar et al. (2015) assert managers collected their share of the rewards by giving themselves large short-term bonuses from the profits tied to these risky investments and cash out their stock options prior to the bank experiencing significant losses from these transactions. One of the suggestions made to curtail this behaviour, Tung (2011) referred to as gamblers' incentive, is to change the compensation framework at the large banks that were identified as significant financial institution by the regulators. This change in the compensation framework would tie bankers' pay to public subordinated debt securities (Tung, 2011). This change in compensation framework would have monitoring controls in place to ensure it carried out as designed, and this would mitigate the risk highlighted by Tung (2011) as equity incentives being used to motivate managers to go overboard and take significant risks at the expense of creditors.

Allen et al. (2016) noted bad investments in high-risk mortgage-backed securities caused many banks to incur significant losses that went undetected in their stress testing activities. Stress testing was introduced by the Federal regulators as a monitoring control activity that would force bank leaders to look at current and potential losses and take mitigating measures to prevent bank insolvency. However, stress test failed to alert bank managers of potential dangers; these test did not predict and prevent losses tied to high risk mortgage-backed securities, high risk trades, or fraudulent banking activities. This was due to the poor design of the stress test. Senior manager's greed pushed them to get involved in risky off-balance-sheet activities to generate increase in earnings (Chang & Talley, 2017). This method was undertaken by managers during periods of lower interest rates to invest in high-risk assets that may garner higher expected returns (Chang & Talley, 2017). Similarly, Hale Balseven (2016) noted large banks tried to maintain their competitive hedge by extending leveraged activities and off-balance-sheet trades. These types of high risk investments were not monitored through effective key controls and key risk indicators. This resulted in significant losses going undetected for long periods of time. The inability to detect significant losses was evident in the use of scenario analysis to perform stress test of many banks. Stress testing should be conducted with other control actives to obtain good results; stress testing by itself is ineffective in predicating losses (Allen et al., 2016). Stress testing should work in concert with control activities that are robust in nature. These controls should cover the rigorous design of the scenario analysis process and scope of coverage (Ong & Pazarbasioglu, 2014). The completeness and accuracy of the underlining data used to perform stress test of bank losses should be subject to key control review; this will help the preparer to feel confident there is no missing data that should be included in the calculations. The significant role data play in stress test is noted by Baker et al. (2015) as key to the model risk design that identifies potential dangerous uncertainties that could cause losses. Legacy software systems and internal bureaucracy have impeded the completeness and accuracy in data quality used in the calculation of stress scenarios (Denev &

Mutnikas, 2016). The calculation of the impact of a stress scenario accuracy relies on the multitude of quantitative models, that is often constrained by internal organizational silos and transparency in the data being used (Denev & Mutnikas, 2016). There are other impediments to the effectiveness of stress test that is aligned with the lack of significant amount of human and monetary resources (Denev & Mutnikas, 2016). Additionally, banks created schemes to manipulate and circumvent the stress testing process results through manipulation of risk-weighted assets and making it harder to detect risk (Glasserman & Tangirala, 2016). There is the added political pressure by lobbyist in Washington who played a role in weakening the stress test process under the guise of high implementation cost (Glasserman & Tangirala, 2016).

However, stress test models are key tools in risk mitigation efforts that quantify risk embedded in financial decision-making (Baker et al., 2015). Independent stress test performed by the regulators of banks capital scenarios reveals that banks are under-capitalized, and they were concerned with the deterioration of selected banks capital position (Kapinos & Mitnik, 2016). The Fed raised concerns rebating the state of several banks capital levels and suggest that these banks will need significant capital injection to keep them afloat (Kapinos & Mitnik, 2016). Capital injections provide a buffer for troubled banks to keep their capital levels above the minimums required by the regulators (Kapinos & Mitnik, 2016). Banks keeping minimum capital levels above the levels set by regulators would require key controls that will prevent losses that will erode capital and monitoring controls to ensure capital levels are meeting the requirements. Key controls could be effective if designed correctly which should incorporate the use of sound risk measurement approach, examine risk embedded in financial decision-making, portfolio and investment planning and taking actions to mitigate identified risk (Baker et al., 2015).

The timeliness of the review, financial health of the bank and external market conditions should be taken into consideration in the preparation of a successful stress testing activity (Ong & Pazarbasioglu, 2014). Significant losses that remain unmitigated can cause banks to go out of business. Ertürk (2016) argues bank manager's efforts to meet shareholder's objectives of lucrative profits caused them to take on high-risk investments in volatile products, led to significant losses, exposing the bank to bankruptcy (Ertürk, 2016). The magnitude of these losses exposed banks with bad leadership to bankruptcy which caused harm to communities and markets domestically and globally. These banks were considered to be significant financial institutions that were given the status of too big to fail. Biljanovska (2016) asserts many banks that suffered significant losses without sufficient capital to continue business should have gone through the federal insolvency laws of winding down the bank. On the contrary, these banks bypass the insolvency laws because they received shelter under the umbrella of too big to fail. Biljanovska (2016) contends these too big to fail banks were seen as a systemic risk because of their size and global reach, received significant government bailouts, that became an incentive for bank leaders to continue with their risk-taking behaviour.

Hence, the Fed used public funds to bail them out and prop them up. The Federal Reserve Bank in this role of being the invisible hand acts as a safety net in the banking industry that prevents banks from going bankrupt. Many banks took advantage of this safety net to boost their confidence when they make risky bets and suffer significant losses; the Fed rescues some of these banks from failure and bankruptcy. Aiyar et al. (2015) mentioned Fed functioning as a safety net provides protection to many banks which prevented them from becoming insolvent and negatively affect the economy. However, this was seen as a moral hazard by Petitjean (2013) who argued that this rescue of failing banks further decays in the sector when central banks and government offer bailouts to troubled banks during a crisis. These moral hazard problems take on legs, and they increase as banks that are too big to fail take on more risk as they rely on government bailouts as a rescue mechanism when they encounter distress (Nisha, 2016). Additionally, Noreen et al. (2016) pointed out the moral hazard behaviour of bank manager should be examined as part of the root causes of the significant losses banks incur; this behaviour is tied to the short-term returns mindset of the managers who bypass the bank's charter value that they should adhere to as agents. Noreen et al. (2016) continue to point to the root causes of these managers' moral hazard behaviour tied to their greed of earning large amounts of short-term profits without no consideration to the future value of the firm (Noreen et al., 2016). Bank managers continue to take high-stake risk because of the government safety nets that will catch them if the bank is in trouble financially.

The federal government acting as a safety net for banks provided them with intrinsic and extrinsic motivation which caused them to take on more high-risk products with the belief that if they were to fail, they would receive bailouts (Dandapani et al., 2017). The Fed tries to protect the economy from the negative impacts of bank runs by offering bailouts to institutions with public money (Pollick et al., 2016). Citizens domestically and globally were not pleased with the act of the Fed bailing out failing banks with public funds that many referred to as tax payers' money. These citizens believed that when they are experiencing financial distress due to poor management of funds, the Fed did not offer them bailouts. The public sentiment was that bad banks with poor internal control systems that were poorly managed should go out of business. This sentiment spread widely domestically and internationally after many witnessed public companies that received bailouts returned to the bad acts. American International Group (AIG) was one these public companies that was deemed by the Fed as too big to fail due to its global reach and catastrophic impact its losses and insolvency would have negative impacts on the global financial markets. Robertson and Sullivan (2009) assert AIG after receipt of government bailout funds returned to paying out performance bonus in the millions to its top leadership and sent top performers in the company to expensive resort trips. This information became public knowledge which caused many global citizens to not support government bailouts.

Globally, this approach of offering bailout to troubled banks using public funds to prevent these losses spilling over into the economy was seen as the solution (Pollick et al., 2016). Many central banks and government regulators embraced this approach despite global citizens frowned on this method of solving bank runs and economic decay. The knock-on effects of pumping bailout funds into these banks was a systemic solution that prevented risk of insolvency, interruption of credit and payment services to customers (Pollick et al., 2016). Government bailout approach is seen as a mandatory needed action from the regulators to solve the problems of failing banks; as such, prudential rights and wiggle room were given as a resolution to authorities to do their job of rescuing failing banks (Davies, 2015). Some of the responsibilities of the government regulators are to monitor trading activities such as insider trading that is tied to significant losses. Montagano (2012) referred to insider trading as a danger to global capital markets that have caused global government bodies to increase regulators' powers to detect and stamp out these practices. There are some financial vehicles referred to as shadow banks that are structurally different from a commercial banks; these shadow banks reap the benefits of government safety-net without the burdens of prudential rules compliance requirements (Crawford, 2017). Commercial banks have to establish controls to ensure it is in compliance with the prudential rules established by the regulators in order to obtain the safety nets provided by the government when faced with significant losses and business continuity troubles. Crawford (2017) mentioned commercial banks are required to remain in compliance with prudential rules. The lax regulatory environment with less compliance requirements for shadow banks caused them to become creative and flexible in their high risk investments. They are very creative in how they diversified their portfolio because of the benefits of the wiggle room they have been afforded. Shadow banks received the benefits of having the Fed functioning as a safety net, and they diversified their asset portfolio with profitable returns (Lin et al., 2018).

The financial burdens many traditional banks incurred to maintain effective control to meet the prudential regulation rules have caused many of them to look into the alternative of operating as a shadow bank. This was evident in many traditional banking activities were transitioned to shadow banking activities that appeared to be lucrative and profitable (Lin et al., 2018). There is the issue of commercial banks who continued to operate traditionally that incurred significant losses and refused to take assistance from the Fed. These banks refrained from taking the helping hand provided by the Fed as they believed this came with a negative stigma in the banking industry that caused customers to lose confidence in them. This negative stigma that banks believed came with taking bailouts from the Fed caused the safety net role played by the Fed to fail. Banks refused to access the discount window to borrow funds when they experienced a crisis because they feared depositors, creditors and their investors would see them as a weak bank (Gorton, 2015). During the 2008 financial crisis, 322 banks became bankrupt and closed up business because they did not receive a bailout from the Fed (Álvarez-Franco & Restrepo-Tobón, 2016). There were many banks who did well and were very resilient to the 2008 financial crisis as they had strong internal control structure. Those banks with weak internal controls experience more significant losses and some became insolvent.

Credit Suisse, one of Switzerland largest bank, experiences significant losses and was exposed to insolvency due to its weak internal control environment and non-functioning internal controls. Government and global central banks rallied to

Credit Suisse rescue to mitigate the insolvency that would be a systemic risk to global financial structure. Large banks such as Credit Suisse size and global reach caused losses incurred to significantly affect their local environment and spread to global markets. These losses that are systemic in nature are Idiosyncratic, and because of their negative impacts and threats to both local and global banking/financial services industry, government regulators intercede to prevent them from insolvency. These losses posed ill effects on global markets as (Berman) 2019 mentioned the negative impacts from the losses eroded the credit metrics, and send volatile shockwaves through the global banking environment. Swiss institutions devised a merger between United Bank of Switzerland (UBS) and Credit Suisse where UBS would buy Credit Suisse for 3 billion Swiss francs ($3.23 billion) and absorb $5.4 billion in losses from the failing Credit Suisse (Suresh & Monalisa, 2024). Several global central banks (Federal Reserve, Bank of Canada, England, Japan, European Central Bank) reacted to the news of Credit Suisse demise by making a public declaration to increase the facility of liquidness to the bank which was a measure to calm frightened customers (Suresh & Monalisa, 2024). Central banks have been known as lender of last resort (LOLR) to commercial banks to provide stability to the commercial banking system (Alexander et al., 2023). On the other hand, Dowd and Hutchinson (2016) saw the role of the central bank as an instigator for risk taking by banks as they expect the central bank to bail them out when they find themselves in trouble. These banks were offered protection from their own ill behaviour that causes failures and consequences tied to their bad decisions-making (Dowd & Hutchinson, 2016). These central banks have widened their focus from providing liquidity insurance to banks to backstopping market liquidity in scenarios where severe dysfunction threatens the banks' financial stability (Alexander et al., 2023). The mitigation of dysfunctional banking environment and fostering stability quells the fears of customer in the markets. Customers reacted to news of their banks experiencing financial woes and possibility of going bankrupt negatively; they ran to the bank to withdraw all their funds. This behaviour could cause bank runs when related/affiliated banks soon find they are exposed to the panic withdrawals from customers and some of knock-on effects from the bank in trouble which can cause them to become insolvent as well. Additionally, the global central bank actions towards Credit Suisse were designed to increase the confidence level of worried lawmakers and investment bankers (Suresh & Monalisa, 2024).

Britain's Barings bank had an international presence where it had a 40% stake in US investment bank Dillon Read which carried on its books an estimated $316 million in reserves (Eldridge & Lynch, 1995). The interconnected nature of these two investment entities makes them vulnerable to losses spreading from one to the other; these losses replicate to the global markets through financial institution they conduct business activities. The interconnected nature of these banks facilitates rapid global spread rate and impact which can be slowed down if both host banks have good internal controls in a strong control environment. A control environment with effective (preventative, detective, monitoring) controls can mitigate system risk that losses posed to business and the exponential spread can be quarantined or prevented from leaking into the financial market sector. Trades are a banking activity that is idiosyncratic in nature, subject to produce significant gains or losses, and the impacts from this event/activity can be felt domestically and globally. Significant trade losses if not mitigated and addressed in a timely manner can cause banks to become insolvent if this weakness persists and not addressed. This type of event occurred at Barings bank. Baring became insolvent when it suffered significant trade losses incurred by a single trader which the bank was unable to cover and the Britain Central bank stepped in to close down the bank (Eldridge & Lynch, 1995). Many of these trades were derivative products which were highly volatile and expose banks to significant losses. The need for regulation of over-the-counter derivatives was heightened during the 2008 global financial crises (Guynn, 2010). Derivatives are highly risky products due to volatile nature of this financial instrument which is often times used as off-balance-sheet trades that are conducted over-the-counter and not publicly traded on an exchange (NASDAQ, NYSE) which was a significant problem for regulators to manage the risk, a regulatory problem (Mohamed, 2015). The regulators in the United States required significant banks that operate domestically and globally to keep derivatives trading activities and credit default swaps into a separate investment vehicle outside of the bank as a means to manage risk exposure to the bank from these high-risk products (Johnson, 2015). A mitigation measure used is to separate capitalized affiliate function by keeping derivatives traded on behalf of customers in a different company (Johnson, 2015). The government regulatory bodies do not back high-risk bank activities that are speculative in nature such as proprietary trades that are high-risk ventures (Johnson, 2015). The Federal Deposit Insurance Corporation requires hedge or private equity funds kept separate from the part of the business that is insured under depository institution requirements (Johnson, 2015). The strong message these regulators are sending to the public is one that highlights that banks should not engage in trading activities to make profit at the risk of its depository customers incurring significant losses (Johnson, 2015). There are strict guidelines that these banks should adhere to, and their failure to comply results in them obtaining findings. The regulators can intercede in how a bank is being managed and place the bank into receivership.

Bank of England assigned Ernst and Young the accounting firm as administrators for Barings bank which is the equivalent to banks in the United States being placed under receivership (Eldridge & Lynch, 1995). This caused a systemic negative reaction in the global markets Tokyo stock exchange's Nikkei 225-stock average dropped 664 points or 3.8% (Eldridge & Lynch, 1995). The regulators and bank executives rely on loss data bases that track internal and external losses in the banking sector. Some voting statements on losses that had low desirability and feasibility ratings from the panel of experts are noted below. These statements votes are displayed in Tables (5–7) (Velez, 2020).

Government rallied to save Credit Suisse and similar measures were applied to save Bank of England. Government officials worked long hours to find buyer for the bank and failed, which they thought would prevent big systemic losses in Tokyo, Hong Kong and London markets (Eldridge & Lynch, 1995). Guynn (2010) echoed the importance of the use of macro-prudential regulatory measures

Table 5. Internal Control Activities ORX Loss Databases 2nd Round Data: Non-consensus.

Statement	Ratings	Total Number of Panelist Who Selected Each Ratings
Statement 14 – Internal control activities towards capital regulation that can be effective in reducing losses includes use of internal and external Operational Risk Exchange (ORX) loss databases to benchmark against industry.		
	Highly undesirable: Will have major negative effect.	2
	Undesirable: Will have a negative effect with little or no positive effect.	0
	Neither desirable nor undesirable: Will have equal positive and negative effects.	3
	Highly desirable: Will have a positive effect and little or no negative effect.	2
	Definitely infeasible: Cannot be implemented (unworkable).	0
	Probably infeasible: Some indication this cannot be implemented.	1
	May or may not be feasible: Contradictory evidence this can be implemented.	0
	Probably feasible: Some indication this can be implemented.	6
	Definitely feasible: Can be implemented.	2

Table 6. Internal Controls Activities Monitoring of Bank Assets 2nd Round Data: Non-consensus.

Statement	**Ratings**	**Total Number of Panelist Who Selected Each Ratings**
Statement 22 – Internal control activities towards capital regulation that can be effective in reducing losses includes compliance and content monitoring of bank assets as well as complete overview of all activities.		
	Undesirable: Will have a negative effect with little or no positive effect.	1
	Neither desirable nor undesirable: Will have equal positive and negative effects.	1
	Desirable: Will have a positive effect with minimum negative effects.	2
	Highly desirable: Will have a positive effect and little or no negative effect.	2
	Definitely infeasible: Cannot be implemented (unworkable).	0
	Probably infeasible: Some indication this cannot be implemented.	0
	May or may not be feasible: Contradictory evidence this can be implemented.	2
	Probably feasible: Some indication this can be implemented.	4
	Definitely feasible: Can be implemented.	5

Table 7. Internal Controls Activities Dual Control of Processes 2nd Round Data: Non-consensus.

Statement	**Ratings**	**Total Number of Panelist Who Selected Each Ratings**
Statement 108 – Internal control activities towards capital regulation that can be effective in reducing losses includes dual control of processes should be implemented or in operation to reduce risk from human errors.		
	Highly undesirable: Will have major negative effect.	1
	Undesirable: Will have a negative effect with little or no positive effect.	0
	Neither desirable nor undesirable: Will have equal positive and negative effects.	2
	Desirable: Will have a positive effect with minimum negative effects.	2
	Highly desirable: Will have a positive effect and little or no negative effect.	1
	Definitely infeasible: Cannot be implemented (unworkable).	1
	Probably infeasible: Some indication this cannot be implemented.	2
	Probably feasible: Some indication this can be implemented.	2
	Definitely feasible: Can be implemented.	4

and supervision laws for winding up too big to fail financial institutions. The Bank of England mentioned the failure to find a buyer to bailout Barings banks is because of the significance of the losses, possibility of millions more in losses from open derivative contracts and significant uncapped liability (Eldridge & Lynch, 1995). Regulators failed to understand the root causes for significant losses banks incurred and this was evident in the case of Barings bank. A weak real estate market contributed to Sovran Bank/Maryland ($4.2 billion subsidiary of C&S/Sovran) lost $16.1 million during the third quarter, which prompted the bank to set aside a $300 million provision to its reserves to absorb future loan losses (Frank, 1991). The provision on the subsidiary book caused the parent company to incur a $50.8 million loss on its books (Frank, 1991). The sour loans that burden the US economy had knock-on effects on State-chartered banks in Maryland which caused it to incur a $23.9 million loss during the third quarter of 1991, and several other large states' institutions showed continuing problems tied to sour loans (Frank, 1991).

The continuous negative economy in the United States caused damage to several banks (Frank, 1991). The weakness of the economy stemming from systemic losses that spread through the global banking sector caused some banks to sell off assets; many Hedge funds and Private Equity benefited from by picking up that business. Arnold and Goff (2014) posit private equity executives discussed the large sums of money purchasing bargains among the assets sold by banks; they saw it as a good to the banking sector as it helped to reduce the losses suffered on sales of non-core portfolios, even allowed lenders to book gains by reducing loss provisions. This was evident where UBS was able to raise EUR200bn to buy distressed real estate assets from European banks; this left the European banks with a remainder of $2.4tn of non-core assets to sell (Arnold & Goff, 2014). The selling of dead weight assets on European banks balance sheet help them stay afloat and have a lighter weight balance sheet contributing to a healthier banking system.

Private Equity, hedge funds, distress debt buyers move into the global financial markets to reap the benefits of the weak market created by bank losses buying up distress debts for cheap. Europe's large, distressed debt investors saw significant increase in their investments in distress debt with a significant remainder of debt left to absorb which ranges from $1tn to $2bn out of their $45tn asset bases that banks have to be relieved (Arnold & Goff, 2014). As noted by Le et al. (2016), troubled banks have benefitted from the transfer of risk from the balance sheet to the capital markets which frees up costly equity capital for other use. Many large banks were forced to refile credit risk as market risk through use of transactions created money through new lending which they did deceitfully bypassing regulators' intended restrictions on securitization (Hanke & Sekerke, 2017). During 2009, the Lloyds bank of England placed over 236bn pounds of assets into its failing bank which dwindled down to 63.5bn pound after a few years; the bank resolved to the release of a significant amount of net capital released from non-core asset sales in the amount of

2.6bn pounds (Arnold & Goff, 2014). The various central banks of Europe have stepped in to assist the failing banks by easing some of the pressures and dead weight debt and losses on many banks' books.

In the United States, Congress intervened in preventing insolvency of large banks due to their significant losses by providing USA Troubled Asset Relief Program (TARP) USD 700 billion bailout funds of which USD 313 billion was disbursed to significant banks (Velez, 2020). On the other hand, the US government allowed Bear Stearns and Lehman Brothers to collapse as a result of their losses from subprime mortgages that went sour (Deos et al., 2015). Fahey (2016) asserts AIG received $182 billion bailout fund from the government which they were able to pay back a short time after and an additional $23 billion (Fahey, 2016). In India, eight large banks reported losses of Rs 53,000 in 20,018; this was linked to stagnant economic growth stemming from the government being unable to repair the stressed balance sheets of Indian companies (AB, 2018). The knock-on effects were visible in corporate loans led by the infrastructure sector which caused banks to shrink their loans to companies that were in the process of cleaning their books and restructuring their business (AB, 2018). Throughout Europe (Greek, Italian, Germany, UK) government lend bad banks a helping hand by putting some of their most toxic assets into non-core divisions (Arnold & Goff, 2014). Spain and Ireland governments use their state bad banks to manage their financial sectors' problem assets and losses as a response to their impacts from the global financial crisis (Arnold & Goff, 2014).

During 2022, Bank of England intervened in the financial markets as lenders of last resort to support UK financial stability through growing market-based finance, use of temporary asset buy/sell tools, which fostered financial stability in a stressful market (Alexander et al., 2023). UK used a resolution initiative through the emergency legislation rescue mechanism Banking Act 2009 to help troubled banks; UK government was able to offer bailout to failing banks (Gordon& Ringe, 2015). The Banking Act 2009 granted authority to the Bank of England powers to put a bank into temporary public ownership (Gordon & Ringe, 2015). The UK government bond market in 2022 had severe dysfunction and liability-driven investment (LDI) funds were removed from company's books through fire-sale dynamics; Bank of England created a temporary backstop facility (Alexander et al., 2023). The Bank of England bought £19.3 billion of gilts (UK Government Bonds) between 28 September and 14 October 2022 which entails £12.1 billion of conventional government bonds and £7.2 billion of index-linked government bonds (Alexander et al., 2023). These government bonds were subsequently sold back to the market in a timely manner over 12 trading days between November 2022 and January 2023 (Alexander et al., 2023). This government intervention to stabilize the market is intended to be a temporary intervention, after which, the market is left to function on its own. Central banks usually have these two tools (lending operations, asset purchases) which are preferred when stabilizing an economy in a financial crisis. Alexander et al. (2023) mentioned central banks respond to severe market dysfunction by use of lending operations that allows banks to use their assets as collateral to borrow liquidity in the form of central bank reserves at a fixed term. Central banks then unwind these asset purchase once the market risk has stabilized; these moves from the central bank prevent fire sales of the troubled bank assets (Alexander et al., 2023). Global governments are of the beliefs that the losses from frauds are tied to weak or laxed internal controls.

Chapter 4

Sarbanes–Oxley (SOX) 2002 and Control Environment

The failure of Enron, one of the largest US companies, drove US government bodies to place emphasis on passing Sarbanes–Oxley (SOX) Act of 2002 laws that would regulate the effectiveness of a company's internal controls (Aksoy & Mohammed, 2020). Enron was a publicly listed company on the New York Stock Exchange with revenues of $111 billion in 2000, and *Fortune* magazine named Enron America's Most Innovative Company for five years spanning from 1995 to 2000 (Thomsen & Norman, 2008). By December 2001, Enron filed for bankruptcy, which was at that time the largest bankruptcy in US history, and evidence revealed Enron's financial reports were inflated with fraudulent accounting numbers (Thomsen & Norman, 2008). The US government believed that the lack of effective functioning internal controls with Enron's control environment caused the company to go out of business. Several major corporate and accounting scandals relating to significant public companies (Enron, Tyco International, Adelphia, Peregrine Systems, WorldCom) caused investors to lose billions of dollars when the share prices of the impacted companies collapsed, and consumers developed negative public confidence in financial securities markets (Act, 2002). This need for SOX controls was further bolstered by fraudulent activities at WorldCom and Tyco which caused Senator Paul Sarbanes and Representative Michael to create the SOX Act of 2002 (Stigliano, 2011). Senate and the House worked tirelessly to implement corporate fraud reform after Enron 2001 bankruptcy following by multi-billion-dollar financial fraudulent activities at (WorldCom, Global Crossing, Adelphia, Xerox, Tyco) companies which led to their collapse (Thomsen & Norman, 2008). Several hearings were held by the Senate Banking Committee on the market problems that constituted losses of billions which spiralled into trillions of dollars in market value (Act, 2002). The results of these hearings led to passing of SOX Act of 2002.

The results of these hearings led to passing of SOX Act of 2002. Sarbanes–Oxley Act of 2002 was enacted 30 July 2002, referred to as Public Company Accounting Reform, known in the Senate as Investor Protection Act', in the house as Corporate and Auditing Accountability and Responsibility, and other popular names (Sarbanes–Oxley, Sarbox, SOX) is a United States Federal Law (Act, 2002). This act

Effective Internal Control Practices in Banks, 49–58

Published under exclusive licence by Emerald Publishing Limited
doi:10.1108/978-1-83662-972-620251004

set new and enhanced standards for US public company boards, management and public accounting firms (Act, 2002). The SOX Act required corporations to modify their accounting methods and actively regulate various stakeholders (auditors, CEO, CFO, Chairman) of public companies (Stigliano, 2011). The act contains 11 Sections: Section 1, Public Company Accounting Oversight Board (PCAOB), provides independent oversight of auditors; Sections 2 establishes standards for external auditor independence/conflicts of interest; Section 3, senior executives, is held responsible for accuracy and completeness of company's financial reports; Section 4 requires internal controls to ensure accuracy of financial reports and audits to be perform on those controls; Section 5 address restoration of investor confidence through defining codes of conduct for securities analysts; Section 6 defines Securities and Exchange Commission's (SEC's) authority to censure/bar securities professionals from practice; Section 7 requires studies relating to effects of consolidation of public accounting firms, credit rating agencies role in the operation of securities markets, securities violations and enforcement actions; Section 8 describes criminal penalties for manipulation/destruction of financial records; Section 9 provides protections for whistleblowers; Section 10 defines corporate fraud and records tampering as criminal offenses with penalties; Section 11 revises sentencing guidelines and penalties (Act, 2002). The Act mostly required by public companies to abide by the various statues defined the internal controls certification and requirements for company's management in its Sections 3 and 4s. SOX Section 3, Corporate Responsibility Title III, has eight sections that require senior executives take individual responsibility for the accuracy and completeness of the financial statements, require interaction between external auditors and audit committees, limit corporate officer's behaviours and outline forfeitures of benefits and penalties for non-compliance (Act, 2002).

In Section 302 of Section 3 of the Act, the Chief Executive Officer (CEO) and Chief Financial Officer (CFO) are required to approve the integrity of their company's financial statements and reports on a quarterly basis (Act, 2002). Section 4, Enhanced Financial Disclosures Title IV, outlines enhanced reporting requirements (financial transactions, off-balance-sheet transactions, pro-forma figures, stock transactions of corporate officers) and internal controls that should attest to the accuracy of financial reports and disclosures (Act, 2002). The CEO and CFO are required under Section 302 to certify quarterly and annually in the respective report that they have reviewed the filing for completeness and accuracy, and to the best of their knowledge, the internal accounting controls of the company are effective (Thomsen & Norman, 2008). CEOs and CFOs are required to reimburse the company under Section 304 for all bonuses and other equity-based compensation they received within 12 months filing a materially non-compliant financial statements that have subsequently restated due to misconduct (Thomsen & Norman, 2008). There are criminal penalties for individuals and firms found to be not in compliance with SOX Act requirement. Additionally, Sarbanes–Oxley Act of 2002 increased criminal provisions to the securities laws; individual jail terms for securities violations changed from 10 to 20 years, fines increased from $1 million to $5 million (Thomsen & Norman, 2008).

These criminal charges are bolstered by SOX Section 802: Criminal penalties for violation of SOX Section 802(a) which stipulates intentional fraudulent actions (alters, destroys, mutilates, conceals, covers up, falsifies, makes a false entry in any record/document/tangible object) to prevent (impede, obstruct, influence) an investigation by agency of the United States will be fined under this title and face imprisonment of up to 20 years (Act, 2002). Also, the Act provisions protect whistleblowers as they are usually on the ground and see first-hand the potential occurrence of fraud and report it to the appropriate authorities.

Whistleblowers are protected in SOX Section 1107 which articulates criminal penalties for retaliation against whistleblowers Section 1107 (Act, 2002). The Act stipulates that an individual who knowingly/intentionally takes retaliation and harmful actions (interference with lawful employment, block livelihood of the person) for giving information to a law enforcement officer about the occurrence or possible committing of a federal offense shall be fined with imprisonment up to 10 years (Act, 2002). The whistleblower programme allows individuals to anonymously report violators or a potential violation of SOX rules to the regulatory bodies often times by calling a toll-free number to report information. Whistleblowers have been instrumental to catching corporate frauds which takes a lot of courage to report fraudulent acts which have been ongoing for many years leading to public scandals for the company (Stigliano, 2011). Audit committees are mandated to establish whistleblower procedures that provide guidelines and steps employees can use to report anonymously concerns about potential fraudulent accounting or auditing actions (Thomsen & Norman, 2008). Ghosh (2021) mentioned company should strengthen their whistleblowing programme to protect the whistleblower and offer empowerment to the department that champions this programme.

Stigliano (2011) contends the purpose and intentions of SOX is to prevent/deter the occurrence of corporate fraud and requires all publicly traded companies to have an audit of their internal control activities by an independent external audit firm. Public companies should implement internal controls activities to facilitate the appropriate capture of recorded individual transactions posted into ending account balances (Stigliano, 2011). Many public companies' filings after the implementation of the SOX Act 2002 had do-overs as they incurred errors in their filings. There was a significant volume of do-overs by public companies listed on the US securities markets to the tune of 1,295 restatements of financial earnings in 2005 which was nearly twice the number for 2004 (Act, 2002). Dodd–Frank Wall Street Reform and Consumer Protection Act 2010 was established by the regulators to address too big to fail organizations, protect consumers from fraud, and wreck less financial institution practices (Haddad & Hakim, 2017). Regulators attempt to address the risks posed by banks with complex operations, diverse activities and volatile products/investments that contributed to bank risk by imposing risk-based capital (RBC) requirements like Basel Norms (Kaur & Kapoor, 2015).

Dodd–Frank Wall Street Reform and Consumer Protection Act 2010 (Dodd–Frank Bill) requires banks in the United States to have internal control activities that ensures the bank maintain Tier 1 capital of 4 % of average consolidated on-balance-sheet assets, a supplementary leverage ratio calibrated using on-balance-sheet assets and off-balance-sheet exposures (Herring, 2016).

Banks will need to use scenario analysis as part of their stress testing activity; the use of macroeconomic scenarios is key to the scenario analysis calculation in capital adequacy stress test computation (Jacobs, 2016). Banks had to create their own macroeconomic scenarios and use statistical model Vector Autoregression (VAR) to quantify data using macroeconomic drivers and modelling segments (Jacobs, 2016). Globally, banks are managing their capital adequacy with varied results where G-10 countries' application of capital regulatory and risk management practices had positive relationship between capital and risk (Kaur & Kapoor, 2015). Banks in Japan had a different experience after implementing capital regulatory practices where the relationship between capital and risk had negative association (Kaur & Kapoor, 2015). France, Italy and the United Kingdom had no significant relationship between capital and risk (Kaur & Kapoor, 2015).

The Dodd–Frank Bill target US banks with $250 billion or greater in assets and foreign exposures more than $10 billion are required to maintain capital requirements; Tier 1 capital should equal a minimum of 3% of the broader denominator, and established monitoring control to ensure it maintains compliance with this requirement (Herring, 2016). Federal Deposit Insurance Corporation (FDIC) created the classification ranges that determine capitalized and not capitalized, noted through the ranges of bank regulatory capital ratios, banks with tier 1 capital ratio greater than 6% are identified as well capitalized (Herring, 2016). Banks have to sustain the capital requirements established by the regulators and periodically submit reports as evidence to regulators that they remain in compliance with five specified minimum capital ratios, at the end of a nine-quarter and severely adverse stress scenario (Herring, 2016). Banks try to manipulate the re-equipment of the regulators while meeting the expectations of shareholders by increasing shareholder wealth by raising their targeted capital ratios and adjusting the composition of portfolios (Kaur & Kapoor, 2015). Banks would change the dynamics of the portfolio by using high-risk assets rather than low-risk weighted assets (Kaur & Kapoor, 2015). Some banks continue to be undercapitalized and engaged in excessive risk (Dowd & Hutchinson, 2016), while other banks take a different approach and have increased their focus on maintaining sound capital adequacy that is in compliance with RBC standards (Kaur & Kapoor, 2015). Banks have been asked to increase their reserves; however as noted by Laiola (2015), capital reserves are not an efficient use of funds. The impacts and relationships between Tier 1 capital requirements and effects to banks' market risk revealed that market risk declined as Tier 1 capital increased (Laiola, 2015). Although the capital reserves benefits are questionable, Hogan and Meredith (2016) mentioned capital ratio can be a good predictor of risk as a compliance measure tool. However, the use of RBC ratio is less reliable as a predictor of risk (Hogan & Meredith, 2016). Banks have engaged in riskier behaviour and the regulation of RBC increases risk in the banking system as it is not able to effectively predict bank risk (Hogan & Meredith, 2016). The supervisory stress testing of Comprehensive Capital Analysis and Review (CCAR) can be inadequate in predicting risk during period of crisis (Jacobs, 2016).

This reporting is completed with the regulator in conjunction with the bank performance of their annual stress tests CCAR and Dodd–Frank Asset Stress Tests (DFAST) (Herring, 2016). There are challenges to the effective application of the Dodd–Frank Bill as noted by Herring (2016) tied to stress testing of capital use of federal regulators risk models that were ineffective and costly, which requires a significant amount of human and monetary resources. Stress test cost linked to data management can be reduced as Kavassalis et al. (2018) assert compliance cost can be reduced through the use of RegTech. Technology can mitigate operational risk linked to inadequate handling of risk data and facilitate effective reporting and cost reduction savings (Kavassalis et al., 2018). RegTech can improve monitoring activities of financial institutions, to identify break down of the reporting system in a timely manner, non-compliant behaviour detection and achieve a high level of risk assessment (Kavassalis et al., 2018). Herring (2016) contends stress test is a necessary and useful compliance activity, but there are drawbacks relating to its complex nature redirected bank executives' focus from mission-critical business objectives to months of data compilation.

SOX helped the SEC uncovered significant fraudulent acts committed by Value line a public filed company on NASDAQ; there were fraudulent actions against its mutual fund shareholders that amounted to $24 million transacted over a period of 20 years (Act, 2002). The fraud was initially reported in the Code of Business Ethics as part of SOX signed by the Value Line Fund portfolio manager to the SEC in 2004 (Act, 2002). Value Line was ordered to pay restitution of $34 million to the impacted Value Line mutual fund investors (Act, 2002). The SOX annual audits that are required to be performed by independent auditors attest to the operating effectiveness of internal SOX controls are then reviewed by the Public Company Accounting Oversight Board (PCAOB or Board). In the Act, the PCAOB is interchangeably referred to as the Board. The PCAOB's responsibilities include overseeing the audit of public companies that are regulated by securities laws to protect the interests of investors and to ensure accuracy in the independent audit reports of the company (Stigliano, 2011). PCAOB Title I of SOX establishes the auditing standards referred to as Auditing Standards 5 (AS 5) to be used by registered public accounting firms also known as external auditors in the preparation of their audit reports (Thomsen & Norman, 2008). The independent external audit firm performs the audit of the company's internal controls to determine if there are weakness in these controls that would contribute to the possibility of occurrence of errors and fraudulent activities (Stigliano, 2011). PCAOB Auditing Standards 5 defines how to comply with SOX Section 404's performance of the internal control's audits. The external audit firms' auditors use a top-down approach as mentioned in Auditing Standards 5 and 2 (AS5, AS2) to execute a risk-based audit approach (Stigliano, 2011). This risk-based approach allows the auditors to understand the public company/auditee business objectives, strategies, business and audit risks, what could go wrong in preparation of financial statements, allows them to document their understanding of internal control and gathers supporting audit evidence (Stigliano, 2011). Thomsen and Norman (2008) assert the PCAOB requires independent external audit firms to retain all audit or review work papers for seven years for all the publicly filed companies they were retained to perform these annual audits. The Act forbids accounting firms (foreign or domestic) that are not registered with the PCAOB from performing audits of US public companies and issuing audit reports, unless they have an exemption (Thomsen & Norman, 2008). The Commission filed on 13 September 2007 39 administrative actions charging 69 audit firms and their partners for performance of financial audits and issuance of report for publicly filed companies while the audit firms have not been registered with the PCAOB (Thomsen & Norman, 2008). The PCAOB is overseen by the SEC. However, there are challenges to the implementation of SOX as many public companies complain about the absorbent cost to implement and monitor the control activities; the audit fees paid to auditors to attest to the functioning control are very costly for the company, and many public companies are looking to go private. The panel of expert's statements related to SOX that had low desirability and feasibility ratings from the panel of experts are noted below. These statements votes are displayed in Tables (8 and 9) (Velez, 2020).

Table 8. Internal Controls SOX Processes 3rd Round Data: Non-consensus.

Statement	**Ratings**	**Total Number of Panelist Who Selected Each Ratings**
Statement 32 – Governance practices senior bank managers can implement towards capital regulation that are effective in reducing losses entails review by internal and external audit of key and SOX processes.		
	Highly undesirable: Will have major negative effect.	0
	Undesirable: Will have a negative effect with little or no positive effect.	2
	Neither desirable nor undesirable: Will have equal positive and negative effects.	2
	Desirable: Will have a positive effect with minimum negative effects.	1

Table 8. *(Continued)*

Statement	Ratings	Total Number of Panelist Who Selected Each Ratings
	Highly desirable: Will have a positive effect and little or no negative effect.	3
	Definitely infeasible: Cannot be implemented (unworkable).	0
	Probably infeasible: Some indication this cannot be implemented.	1
	May or may not be feasible: Contradictory evidence this can be implemented.	0
	Probably feasible: Some indication this can be implemented.	1
	Definitely feasible: Can be implemented.	7

Table 9. Internal Controls (COSO, SOX Basel 111) 3rd Round Data: Non-consensus.

Statement	Ratings	Total Number of Panelist Who Selected Each Ratings
Statement 33 – Risk management practices towards capital regulation that can be effective in reducing losses includes best practices in financial risk management (COSO, SOX, BASEL III, etc.).		

(Continued)

Table 9. *(Continued)*

Statement	**Ratings**	**Total Number of Panelist Who Selected Each Ratings**
	Highly undesirable: Will have major negative effect.	0
	Undesirable: Will have a negative effect with little or no positive effect.	1
	Neither desirable nor undesirable: Will have equal positive and negative effects.	1
	Desirable: Will have a positive effect with minimum negative effects.	3
	Highly desirable: Will have a positive effect and little or no negative effect.	2
	Definitely infeasible: Cannot be implemented (unworkable).	0
	Probably infeasible: Some indication this cannot be implemented.	1
	May or may not be feasible: Contradictory evidence this can be implemented.	0
	Probably feasible: Some indication this can be implemented.	5
	Definitely feasible: Can be implemented.	4

The PCAOB performs periodic inspection of these external audit firms and selects some of the client audits performed for review and to determine compliance with AS 5. The PCAOB conducts investigations and review of audits performed by the external audit firms. The investigation results of these reviews may result in the PCAOB imposing disciplinary actions, corrective sanctions upon registered public accounting firms and their respective employees if they violate the Act and published requirements for compliance (Thomsen & Norman, 2008). The measures outlined by the PCAOB in the Act and provisions of the securities laws related to preparation and issuance of audit reports are to be followed by the external audit firms (Thomsen & Norman, 2008). There are stipulations relating to services external auditors many not provide to publicly filed companies under particular scenarios where they are also performing the independent audit of the financial statements and controls. There are services that external audit firms are prohibited from providing when they are performing an independent audit of the firm's financial and controls which falls into 8 categories: (1) bookkeeping/accounting records or financial statements services of the issuer; (2) IT work which entails financial information systems design and implementation; (3) appraisal/valuation services, fairness opinions or contribution-in-kind reports; (4) actuarial services; (5) internal audit outsource; (6) human resources (HR) and management functions; (7) broker, dealer, investment adviser, investment banking services; (8) legal services and expert services that is not relating to the annual audit (Thomsen & Norman, 2008). Several external audit firms and their associated auditors have been found to be in violation of the PCAOB requirements and were succumbed to disciplinary actions.

The PCAOB brought 16 disciplinary actions against several auditing firms and/or accountants (Thomsen & Norman, 2008). Many audit firms have committed conflict of interest which was never regulated prior to SOX. Before SOX, audit firms self-regulated themselves, and they oftentimes provide audit services for firms they performed significant consulting work (Act, 2002). The consulting agreements paid more fees than the auditing engagement and were considered to be more profitable engagements which was a conflict of interest (Act, 2002). Audit firms are very reluctant to challenge the company's accounting approach as they are concerned this might have a negative impact on the relationship they have with the client (Act, 2002). They are concerned about jeopardizing their lucrative consulting project and future prospects of getting more deals and referrals. As such, an accounting approach that poses a high risk to the company is sometimes carefully presented as low risk with careful delivery to the company so as to not alarm or disturb the company's management. As noted in the Act (2002), audit firms are concerned about damaging their relationship with their clients, placing consulting arrangement at risk and a detriment to the audit firm's bottom line. There is other conflict of interest evident in the securities analysts' roles (acts as purchasers and sellers of company stocks and bonds, investment bankers, provide companies loans, handle mergers and acquisitions) where they wear many hats that make them expose to the conflict of interest (Act, 2002).

Section of 3 of SOX discusses the company's executive responsibility for the accuracy of the financial statements and internal controls activities; the Board of Directors (BOD) is a part of the executive branch of the corporation. The boards of directors and its Audit Committees are commissioned to establish oversight policies and procedures for financial reporting in US companies as stakeholders on the behalf of investors (Act, 2002). The Board of Directors usually consists of 15 members (chairperson, three executive directors, seven non-executive directors, and four independent directors); they work in concert with their various committees (the Strategic Development Committee, Audit Committee, Risk Policy Committee, Personnel and Remuneration Committee, Connected Transaction Control Committee) to oversees the company policies and procedures (Higgins, 2012). The BOD structures that are independent of Audit Committees in the United States are expected to monitor corporate accounting processes; however, in Japan, board members are inside directors who were promoted from within the firm (Hideaki & Naoki, 2021). Senior Management (president, vice-president, other management members) and the various committees report to the BOD; these committees oversee various processes within the business (corporate banking, personal banking, global markets business, operational service, risk management, internal control, securities investment management, purchases, asset disposal, anti-money laundering) and ensure the execution of the activities within these processes are in compliance with SOX (Higgins, 2012). The audit board of significant firms approves the appointment of the external audit firms prior to the shareholders meeting (Hideaki & Naoki, 2021). The external auditors perform an audit of the firm's financial statement and internal control and submit their financial reports to the BOD and the audit board (Hideaki & Naoki, 2021). Audit board members relate their commentaries and concern at the shareholders meeting in relation to their audit of the reporting process and results (Hideaki & Naoki, 2021). There are numerous scandals pertaining to BOD members which have pointed to the BOD as part of the root cause of the failure of these companies.

These scandals identified board members who failed to carry out their duties and/or do not have the knowledge and capabilities to understand the complexities of the businesses (Act, 2002). An ineffective board and its committees contributed to many company scandals because they failed to supervise management (Al-Matari et al., 2017). An example of this behaviour by the board occurred at Enron where the board was complicit in keeping the inaccurate financial statements that were manipulated through the use of off-balance-sheet financing because they were not independent from senior management (Al-Matari et al., 2017). The Board need to have clearly defined roles, communication, and understanding of its responsibilities with stakeholders in order for it to execute effective corporate governance (Bezo & Dibra, 2023).

Part 2

Government SOX Regulations of Banks and SIFIs' Control Environment

Chapter 5

Importance of Effective Internal Control to Company's Control Environment

The US regulatory bodies stated that internal controls can have positive effects on the quality of public companies financial reporting process; the aims of the Sarbanes–Oxley Act 2002 (SOX) guidelines are directed towards the improvement in the internal control activities of publicly listed companies (Hamed, 2023). In concurrence, Hideaki and Naoki (2021) mentioned the accuracy and completeness of a company's financial reporting depends on the effectiveness of Internal Control Systems (ICS), while companies with weak monitoring systems can incentivize managers to commit accounting fraud. Companies that function in an effective internal control environment obtain legitimacy universally by having high-quality ICS/activities, adaptable to the requirements of regulations, norms, display flexibility and mitigate global compliance risks (Chen et al., 2023). Banks have analyzed internal control risk in their accounting practices as part of their approach to implement improved risk control measures; this initiative of mitigating risk is carried out in concert with daily management and operation controls that are effective (Shi & Wang, 2014). An effective internal control environment is required to prevent, detect and monitor corporate misconduct (Chen et al., 2023). Corporate misconduct was heavily displayed in the 2008 financial crisis where there were significant displays of multiple principal–agent problems, information asymmetry, moral hazard, mortgage fraud and risk shifting (Lui, 2011).

The principal–agent problems caused misalignment of party's incentives which instigated risk behaviour in management as displayed in their investment choices (Lui, 2011). The lack of effective preventive control allowed managers to continue with their high risk activities, excessive leverage, and the issuance of bad loans that resulted in significant losses (Lui, 2011). Banks have to gain understanding of embedded risks in principal and agent theory in order for them to design activities to curtail these risks. There are intrinsic and extrinsic motivational factors that push agents to pursue self-gains that are short-term reward but on the long terms create significant losses (Darayseh & Chazi, 2018). Agents have increased their wealth and personal income which have increased the risk exposure of banks due to their high-risk activities as agents (Darayseh & Chazi, 2018).

Effective Internal Control Practices in Banks, 61–79

Published under exclusive licence by Emerald Publishing Limited
doi:10.1108/978-1-83662-972-620251007

There is the unmitigated risk embedded in information asymmetry that posed a risk to banks' sharing of information in a timely manner. This is reflected in the demands for non-financial reporting disclosure required to make social performance decisions that corporate reporting is unable to produce due to lack of clarity and complete information; this has caused banks to have delays in them meeting the needs of the investment community (Stubbs & Higgins, 2018). The quality of the corporate reports lacks clarity, fragmented, complex and often times inadequate for decision-making (Stubbs & Higgins, 2018). The Board of Directors (BOD) have influence over policies and procedures which is a part of the ICS which influence the quality of financial reports. The quality of the Board is influenced by the design of the panel and board members. Nabil (2024) asserts board performance rests on independence, expertise and competence which manifest in effective governance. The opposite scenario is where an organizations' BOD financially illiterate, unintelligent which has contributed to poor financial reporting (Nabil, 2024). This poor financial reporting is a prominent root cause of information asymmetry.

Banks with good governance and internal controls information are adequate and are not plagued by information asymmetry (Abou-El-Sood, 2017). These banks exercise key control activities that strengthen the control environment, help reduce and pre-empt risky behaviour of managers that over time caused the bank to incur significant losses that tend to spread in an interconnected environment. The mitigation of risks stemming from managers behaviour may help promote financial soundness and trust and strengthens banks in the long term. The identification of effective internal control practices in banks can affect banks' functioning in a routine ethical environment, instead of one plague fire drills, and runs on a project mode. Senior bank managers can develop principles that can reduce the level of risk behaviour, while meeting capital requirement and shareholder objectives. ICS can strengthen the internal control framework and weaken information asymmetry risk, which reduces the probability of illegal acts; those illegal acts when committed have a higher discovery rate and investigation, which plays a role in preventing overseas compliance risks (Chen et al., 2023). Management has to identify effective risk management practices and timely implement them to mitigate the growing bank risk that can force banks out of business (McConnell, 2012). Good key controls targeted at creating a moral and ethical culture which will eventually improve risk management (McConnell, 2012). A part of designing a good internal control environment should encompass a risk management framework that should addresses risk gaps (modelling, measuring, managing) that regulators and institutions are required to mitigate; the failure to acknowledge these three factors can erode banks strides towards good risk management practices (Handorf, 2017). Regulators understanding of bank risk processes is necessary for the success and identification of the right modification techniques; this will effect desirable behavioural change, and implementation strategies that work (Viljanen, 2016). The blend of governance, risk management and compliance can improve the internal control environment and ultimately improve effectiveness and efficiency performance (Bezzina et al., 2014). Banks have unresolved issues on measure to address operational risk, significant losses and risky management behaviour in banks (Berger et al., 2018; Dowd & Hutchinson, 2016). The need for internal control activities that addresses change management, technology and self-assessment can improve banks' performance and mitigate behavioural risks exhibited by senior managers' practices. Fischer (2015) asserts self-assessment can improve use of limited resources, improve oversight and develop best practices while reducing significant losses.

Technology and automation of the key processes that is leverage for stress testing can help businesses comply with regulatory filings in a timely manner and reduce time and cost burden associated with these regulations (Meager, 2017). This should be incorporated with information technology controls that prevent, detect, monitor and automate the process. RegTech has been a key recommendation that can be used by banks when there is automation of mass administrative tasks imposed by the regulatory environment (Meager, 2017). Banks are the highest benefactors of RegTech as this is primarily useful in areas of prudential risk management, compliance, capital optimization, trading, portfolio management and cybersecurity (Lai, 2018). Denev and Mutnikas (2016), Dowd and Hutchinson (2016) and Herring (2016) agreed that stress testing of capital through use of federal regulators risk models has been ineffective and costly; the nature of running stress test is cumbersome and requires a significant amount of human and monetary resources. The use of stress testing, and loss- and resource-estimation methodologies have received doubt from bank management. Stress test overall needs improvement which will require effective monitoring and detective controls in place to review the credibility and reliability of stress test. Stress test should be performed in a timely manner with information distributed to stakeholder during the established assigned time; this will allow stakeholder to detect risk early and make the necessary changes to address risk. Kolari and Ivan (2017) see the Basel standards over tress tests as viable recommendation measures for bank. Ong and Pazarbasioglu (2014) argues stress tests must be rigorous in scope, coverage, and scenario design which should capture the health of the bank. To achieve this objective of rigorous scope, targeted key controls have to be designed to meet this initiative. Herring (2016) and Lee (2015) are of the belief that stress test is a useful compliance activity, but it has downfalls due to its onerous nature that pulls bank executives away from mission-critical business objectives. These executives' focus is not on generating profits and meeting shareholders objectives; instead, their focus is pivoted to several months of data compilation (Lee, 2015). Basel Committee proposal for capital limits and stress test requirements and the use of models generated voluminous pages of new regulations, and supervisory practices (Lee, 2015).

Banks' stress test plays a role in capital structure and risk appetite which Kapinos and Mitnik (2016) think capital regulation law should identify acceptable ways to conduct the stress tests of capital. There is the issue of data management that needs considerations when designing effective key controls to mitigate banks risks and losses. The completeness and accuracy of data should be factored into the risk identification process. Data management was highlighted as an area banks should place focus as noted by Alampalli (2013) that accessibility to data can impede the company efforts to meet requirements. Regulatory data are on separate information systems without accessibility to the teams; this caused increased lags in time required by teams to share information (Alampalli, 2013). There need to be flexibility and adaptability of banks to a continuous changing and evolving financial system; however, the regulatory tools and data collection methods were not on par to meet these changes (Alampalli, 2013). There is known frustration with the demand for information and systems capabilities among stakeholders of the process. Arner et al. (2017) assert the automation of processes can be beneficial to risk identification in banks while meeting the regulatory compliance requirements. Financial institutions and regulators can monitor and analyze real-time financial information globally; this can underpin a safer and more efficient financial system (Meager, 2017). Technology paired with effective key automated controls can help businesses with regulation compliance requirements and reduce time and cost burden associated with these regulations in a safe control environment (Meager, 2017). The viewpoint towards the issue of data management is depicted by Meager (2017) that system developments are of little use to banks unless they serve a business purpose and the automation of mass administrative tasks imposed by the regulatory environment. Loss databases used in scenario analysis/stress test need key controls designed to address completeness and accuracy of the data, timely monthly/quarterly reporting, effective use of internal and external risk loss databases provided by Operational Risk Exchange (ORX) and change management practices. Bank managers should establish key controls that give comfort on the completeness and accuracy of the data provided by ORX. Goldberg (2017) underscores the importance of an ecosystem's risk stems from market data and databases, computer and non-automated systems, assumptions and calculations, business decisions, developers, humans and computer programs. There is embedded risk that lies in the use of internal and external risk loss databases provided by ORX to benchmark against their industry, monitoring of bank assets, loss projections and risk exposures. Banks need a strong technological infrastructure that is sustainable through good functioning key preventative and monitoring controls; this will improve the reliance on the data quality and availability that can achieve effective compliance (Boora & Kavita, 2018). There needs to be continuous improvement of dual control processes and operation to reduce human errors. Lai (2018) posits banks face challenges with new and amended regulations compliance, and meeting the reporting time constraints enforced by Basel Committee's. System automation backed by general computer controls, automation of processes, reduction of manual intervention, can meet the committee's guidelines on bank risk data aggregation (Lai, 2018).

Banks can use UIPath Robot processing to automate key processes, which is a viable option. Scenarios analysis, compliance tools, standards and metrics (score card/dash board), key risk indicators are good internal control practices for banks. Bellof and Wehn (2018) and Crabb (2018) pointed out there needs to be improvements made to scenarios that lack transparency and areas of model risk that requires further investigation. There are estimation errors, parameter uncertainties caused by algorithmic methods, use of statistics, computational estimators used in the model framework that need improvement (Bellof & Wehn,

2018). Banks should examine individual model assumptions, variations used in the algorithm, challenger models replaced by alternative model algorithm assumptions which improve the assessment of model risk (Bellof & Wehn, 2018). Lee (2015) asserts linking scenarios and stress-testing processes can capture the bank's material exposures and activities and employ sound activities and approaches that can reduce risk. Third-party risk assessment and modelling tools can greatly assist with compliance, reduce risk levels and mitigate losses (Lee, 2015). This can help to alleviate the difficulties in financial tools such as models used to analyze the relationship between the financial conditions of banks' intermediaries (Fukuda, 2016). There are varied viewpoints toward the issue of tools use to meet banking regulations without paired effective key controls around compliance metrics and analysis tools. Goldberg (2017) pointed out that assurance and compliance measures require banks to have model validation teams with segregation of duties. This requires different roles for model risk managers who develop models, controls and compliance (Goldberg, 2017).

This will eliminate doubts on the reliance on periodic assessment of compliance metrics. Nitescu and Duna (2016) state that effective management of risk, capital and financial system requires compliance at the systemic level. There is risk embedded in customer information and protection of the organization that should be managed through safeguard of information controls. Bank managers express safeguarding of customer information through a robust cyber security program that is proactive is one that needs improvements. This lends support to the assertions of Boora and Kavita (2018) that banks need a strong technological infrastructure, data quality improvements, availability and upgrades that can achieve effective compliance. Boora and Kavita (2018) highlighted important risk management initiatives; risk management controls, tools that safeguard customer information through, and a robust cyber security program that is proactive. This strengthens considerations to use technology as an initiative to safeguard customer information through risk management practices. Lai (2018) suggests RegTech being useful to banks in areas such as risk management, compliance, capital optimization, trading, portfolio management, cybersecurity. Banks' comprehensive enterprise-wide risk management framework was highlighted as key to banks' control environment (Baker et al., 2015). Baker et al. (2015) assert that a risk management framework should consider modelling, measuring and managing that will enable a firm to cope with risk during times that are normal and crisis. Baker et al. (2015) work by drawing attention to important considerations that should accompany risk management in banking in having a comprehensive enterprise-wide risk management framework that includes daily activities.

The use of an enterprise-wide risk management framework should be broad enough to cover all areas of risk and very detail in nature to function as an effective risk management practice. Baker et al. (2015) contend that risk mitigation should incorporate model risk measures and identify economically dangerous uncertainties and risk factors. Banks should exercise a quantitative assessment and risk measurement approach when assessing risk embedded in financial decision-making, portfolio and investment planning (Baker et al., 2015). Periodic risk and control assessment is necessary for banks to improve their internal control environment. Banks should ensure remediation measures are conducted timely to address issues identified in the control basement process. Effective internal control importance is emphasized by Allen et al. (2016) that control activities enhanced through capital regulations requirements of the Dodd–Frank Wall Street Reform and Consumer Protection Act (DFA) 2010 can contain systemic risk and foster financial stability. Allen et al. (2016) draw attention to important considerations that should accompany control activities, including: (a) a periodic risk and controls assessment. Controls should be assessed and measured periodically to ensure effectiveness in meeting regulatory requirements and managing risk. Herring (2016) states banks must demonstrate to regulators their ability to remain in compliance with five specified minimum capital ratios requirements. The internal control activities and objectives of regulators include intervention with banks that fall below minimum capital requirement (Abou-El-Sood, 2017).

Performance evaluation with recommendations for process improvements is important to have in place and install quality measurement in place. This is demonstrated in the assertion of Forrer and Forrer (2015) that bank shareholders and managers have competing views in relation on when to adopt financial innovations. Bank managers are under constant pressure from shareholder to improve performances. Forrer and Forrer (2015) contend that there are important considerations that should accompany quality measures, including: (a) periodic performance evaluation with recommendations for process improvements. There is a correlation between risk and reward that bank shareholders and managers utilized to take excessive risks (Biljanovska, 2016). Regulatory compliance practices are important measures to have in place echoed by Boora and Kavita (2018) that compliance guidance requires banks to develop effective strategies and policies to comply with capital adequacy requirements of Basel III. This is mandatory for banks to become Basel-compliant. Boora and Kavita (2018) mention important considerations that should accompany compliance measures, including: (a) emphasis placed on understanding regulatory compliance, (b) maintenance of effective and independent compliance aligns to organizational objectives, (c) clear definition of data source for compliance analytics. There is emphasis placed on meeting compliance requirements through through various activities such as; understanding regulatory compliance, align compliance goals to business objectives, and clarity in compliance analytical tools used to measure effectiveness of these compliance initiatives.

Goldberg (2017) stipulates that banks should have controls and compliance measurements in place as part of their organizational structure. Risk identification and Basel III faced some scepticism noted by Deos et al. (2015) around Basel III influencing bankers to go back into shadow-banking activities to generate more profits or lower cost operations. In contrast, Gastón and Schumacher (2017) state that Basel III could decrease the probabilities of default for banks, reduce default risk during a crisis episode and over time reduce the idiosyncratic losses. This is an accurate depiction of internal control measure that needs to be in place as depicted by Boora and Kavita (2018); the risk identification has several factors that need to be implemented to make to foster effective risk management efforts such as: nation needs additional funds, capable humans, resources for proper implementation of these norms, strong capital base of banks. Basel III and risk identification with strong key controls would be seen as ineffective doubtful exercises when they are not automated. Handorf (2017) asserts that initiatives around liquidity management without proper controls will continue to fall short of its goals to cure bank default risk. There are liquidity requirements highlighted in Basel III and Dodd Frank Bill 2010 that have received mixed review. These liquidity requirements focus on liquidity risk management, liquidity stress testing and risk profile of the banks. Nitescu and Duna (2016) stress the capabilities that management of liquidity of assets and liabilities of the bank can be effective measures. There is an assortment of viewpoints toward the issue of liquidity stress testing and risk management efforts to monitor economic climate such as trading.

Abou-El-Sood (2017) and Boora and Kavita (2018) both assert that risk management is a good governance regulatory tool banks can utilize to mitigate excessive risk-taking during times of economic turmoil and benefit from risky opportunities in the market during the upside of the economy. Basel-III norms intentions are to increase the resiliency of banks through effective risk management practices. Abou-El-Sood (2017) and Boora and Kavita (2018) draw attention to important considerations that should accompany risk management in banking, including: (a) risk management efforts that monitor economic climate such as trading. Banks need to exercise considerations to the lack of proactive, flexible, adaptive management practices to varied trading climate and data security of client information that can derail risk management initiatives. Kaur and Kapoor (2015), and Walaa and Tucker (2016) state risk management efforts have to be sensitive to the country's economic freedom and policies that enforce stronger mandatory requirements to ensure legitimate banking activities. There should be attention given to the legal systems and needed improvements for independent risk management efforts to overcome bank risk exposure from laws. G-10 countries who implemented risk management and capital regulatory practices had positive relationship between capital and risk and fraud control efforts (Lui, 2011). Banks' risk scope should focus in the embedded risk in mortgage products as noted by Lui (2011) that mortgage fraud, predatory lending, managerial slack and risk shifting and the issuance of bad loans are linked to a weak risk management environment, that caused the financial crisis. Lui (2011) highlights considerations that should accompany risk management in banking, including: (a) risk management efforts aimed at controlling fraud, (b) going above and beyond the minimum risk assessment requirements set forth by the banking regulators (Federal Reserve and Office of the Controller of the Currency). There should be internal controls linked to considerations that will mitigate the lack of risk assessment targeted at fraud control and exceeding the minimum levels set by the bank regulators, which may fail to detect and prevent fraud. As noted by Montagano (2012), market regulators believed that insider trading fraud is harmful to the capital markets domestically and globally.

Risk mitigation should incorporate designing controls to prevent, detect and monitor risk embedded in financial decision-making, portfolio and investment planning, process owners management activities that can mitigate or to alleviate the risk consequences (Baker et al., 2015). There should be training of respective employees which should be a priority for management. Boora and Kavita (2018) note this is essential to keep up with these Basel III norms; banks need to upgrade the skills of their employees by enforcing mandatory training; regulators should consider providing technical support to banks for effective compliance of Basel III. Boora and Kavita (2018) highlight important practices that should accompany risk management in banks including: (a) employee training on bank regulations and (b) compliance training. These considerations should be monitored by implementing key controls to ensure employees are attending key training that is mandatory. Banks that have key employees that lack knowledge updates to keep on top of changes to regulations in relation to compliance and banking regulation can railroad the efforts to curtail bank risk. Denev and Mutnikas (2016) asserts stress testing is not an easy task that requires up to date knowledge obtained through training. There are challenges to employees' performance of these stress test embedded in internal organizational silos and bureaucracy. There should be considerations given to the automation of manual processes that are prone to human errors. This is highlighted in the assertions of Bellof and Wehn (2018) that another form of challenge banks face is human errors incurred during the implementation of models, use of models which can cause operational risk, increase in risk activities to the model risk process caused by conscious selection of assumptions which is a selection risk in itself.

Risk models requires prerequisite review that uncovers dependency existence which can be a key control measure exercise; this practice if used prior to the 2008 recession may have detected embedded high risks in the subprime mortgage. Bellof and Wehn (2018) highlight important considerations that should accompany curtailing human errors in banking, including: (a) use of technology to automate manual processes that are prone to human errors and (b) ensuring employees have time to recognize problems and follow procedures. Banks should consider rolling out the automation of manual processes which will reduce human errors, allow employee more time to review their work and perform quality controls reviews that will identify and correct errors due to less time spent on manual product and more time reviewing their work (Bellof & Wehn, 2018). As noted by Bellof and Wehn (2018), estimation errors and parameter uncertainties caused by algorithmic methods use of statistics are areas of model risk requires further investigation measures to improve reliance on this key control activity. Bank culture that promotes risk-taking within their framework of pre-specified tolerances tends to have less losses or manageable lose in their tolerable limits. The occurrence of unmitigated losses can expose the banks to insolvency risk which lends support to the assertions of Eastburn and Sharland (2017) that growing bank risk can force banks out of business. These risks events will eventually spill over negatively into the economy; increased risk events can be prevented in a respectable risk culture that informs all financial risk-taking and managerial decisions (Eastburn & Sharland, 2017). Eastburn and Sharland (2017) placed emphasis on important considerations that should accompany risk culture in bank, including: (a) use of a framework of pre-specified tolerances and

(b) leaders leading by examples. These considerations need established key controls to enforce their sustainability of having a pre-established framework, pre-specified tolerances for employees to follow, leaders leading by examples through putting initiatives into practice can improve the risk culture within the bank (Eastburn & Sharland, 2017).

Gatzert and Schmit (2016) assert risk culture–backed effective key controls can enforce practices that can influence positive bank activities, reduce senior manager's investment in high risk products, selection of conservative investments and display mindfulness behaviour. Banks that exhibit a risk culture with high levels of morals and integrity may heightened bank managers ethical awareness choices; this could reduce fraudulent behaviors, and business losses (Gatzert & Schmit, 2016). Bank leadership should champion code of ethics and strong morals, and integrity is necessary to an effective control environment. Tourigny et al. (2003) posit the lack of exhibited behaviour reflecting principles of governance and ethical standards has caused bank failures. Noreen et al. (2016) concluded that regulatory authorities should work on ways to control the moral hazard behaviour of bank managers. Noreen et al. (2016) and Tourigny et al. (2003) both highlight significant activities that need enforcement of key controls for sustainability which should accompany ethics in bank, including: (a) the right products for clients and (b) leadership champion of code of ethics, and strong morals and integrity. The practices in banks can garner behaviour which reflects leadership being champion of moral and integrity, as displayed in ethical behaviour reflecting conservative product choices for their clients (Lui, 2011). As noted by Lui (2011), when bank managers lack morals and ethics, this is displayed in their decision-making process; they oftentimes pursue their own financial gains while exposing shareholders to significant losses from their high-risk choice of investments.

Banks that have strong board oversight have displayed in their day-to-day operational activities backed by policies and procedures. Crabb (2018) posits when boards of directors do not have information needed to make informed decisions, the bank tends to suffer from this weakness. Goldberg (2017) states that banks are required to have governance and control mechanisms in place, board and senior management oversight, policies and procedures, controls and compliance and an appropriate incentive and organizational structure. There are mixed viewpoints toward board oversight as noted that board structure can be a weakness to bank decision-making process due to its size. The issue depicted by O'Sullivan et al. (2016) is that during a crisis, banks with large board experience bottlenecks and hindrance with timely risk management decisions. To improve the process, banks should address board structure before there is a crisis; there is a link between board size, CEO and board tenure, the increase in bank performance and the lowering of bank risk (O'Sullivan et al., 2016). The implication is that banks can experience improvements in risk levels when there are active board oversight, small boards, long-term tenure that can be effective in its oversight role of the bank. The risk mitigation framework coupled with well-designed key controls and key risk indicators can identify economically dangerous uncertainties and their risk factors, emerging risk and risk embedded in financial decision-making that can make the bank vulnerable to insolvency (Baker et al., 2015). Senior managers' investment in high-risk products can be reduced by enforcing preventative and monitoring controls around high-risk products, which will essentially force them to select less risky investments. Bank managers should heighten their risk awareness through training that covers ethical awareness choices, thereby reducing fraudulent behaviours, and decrease business losses stemming from errors and fraud (Gatzert & Schmit, 2016). Banks' risk that is idiosyncratic in nature can force banks out of business and eventually spill over negatively into the local and global economy if left unmitigated, which causes another recession. The increase of risk can be prevented in a respectable risk culture, that has a thorough review process prior to financial risk-taking and managerial decisions (Eastburn & Sharland, 2017).

Banks with effective internal control improve operational transparency which alleviates information asymmetry and acts as a deterrence to violations and managers' self-interested behaviours (Chen et al., 2023). The increase in the integrity of all forms of information through having adequate internal controls can aid in the long-term growth of firms with a high level of predictability, consistency and confidence (Hamed, 2023). There are several benefits to a company's financial health tied to the effectiveness of its ICS. For example, ICS's benefits to a company include facilitation of consistent and accurate financial reporting and assurance in the achievement of the firm's objectives and enable meeting the demands of providing timely information to internal and external stakeholders (Hamed, 2023). ICS fosters economic progress and improvement to the banking sector flawed by sluggish growth, unstable macroeconomic activities plagued by risk of fraud and corruption (Hamed, 2023). Moreover, ICS has proven to have positive impacts on the environmental, social and governance (ESG) ratings, which is a good indicator of corporate sustainability; a well-designed ICS enhanced operational efficiency and effectiveness, reliable reporting and compliance to respective laws and regulations (Hamed, 2023). An ICS that is well designed (systematic, complete, rigorous, quick responding) can mitigate supervision loopholes and compliance risk (Chen et al., 2023). The use of ICS can reduce conditions favourable to non-compliance, internal control weakness and opportunistic managers' behaviour (Chen et al., 2023). A well-designed ICS system will require all employees to become stakeholder of practising good effective internal controls that operate in a segregation of controls environment. This makes it difficult for collusion and management override of the system. Bezo and Dibra (2023) noted a successful internal control programme requires the participation of all employees and management at all levels in the organization. It is essential for management to exercise competence and professional integrity which are necessary components of a sound internal control program; management should establish adequate policies and procedures which layout acceptable activities for processing transactions that are aligned with regulations (Bezo & Dibra, 2023).

Al-Hawatmeh (2021) contends internal controls success is based on its design which entails five elements (control environment, risk assessment, control activities, information and communication and monitoring). Hamed (2023) noted control activities, information and communication and monitoring are key segments of ICS that are key drivers of bank performance. Velez (2020) noted that a strong control environment is one that has controls designed (prevent, detect, monitor) to mitigate errors or fraud; controls put stops in place to ensure proper authorization is completed before execution of transactions. Banks that have strong governance committees, reporting and escalation, and establish periodic risk and controls assessment have a strong ICS (Velez, 2020). The Committee of Sponsoring Organizations of the Treadway Commission (COSO) Framework has been used by internal management and external auditors to assess a well design internal control framework. The COSO 2013 provides a framework for designing an internal control environment which underscored the important components (control environment, risk assessment, control activities, information and communication, monitoring) that are necessary to mitigate risks and fraud (Hamed, 2023). Hamed (2023) noted risk assessment is used to identify potential and current risk that could prevent companies from achieving their goals and objectives and using this information as a basis of determining how to manage these risks. The votes on risk assessment, control activities, information and communication and monitoring activities varies. There are some risk assessments controls activities votes that resulted in non-consensus which had 5 votes or less, while some assessment activities had 6 votes or more meeting consensus. These statements votes are displayed in Tables (10–15) (Velez, 2020).

Table 10. Internal Controls Periodic Risk and Controls Assessment 3rd Round Data: Consensus.

Statement	Ratings	Total Number of Panelist Who Selected Each Ratings
Statement 44 – Internal control activities towards capital regulation that can be effective in reducing losses includes periodic risk and controls assessment.		
	Highly undesirable: Will have major negative effect.	0
	Undesirable: Will have a negative effect with little or no positive effect.	0
	Neither desirable nor undesirable: Will have equal positive and negative effects.	2

(Continued)

Table 10. *(Continued)*

Statement	Ratings	Total Number of Panelist Who Selected Each Ratings
	Desirable: Will have a positive effect with minimum negative effects.	4
	Highly desirable: Will have a positive effect and little or no negative effect.	6
	Definitely infeasible: Cannot be implemented (unworkable).	1
	Probably infeasible: Some indication this cannot be implemented.	0
	May or may not be feasible: Contradictory evidence this can be implemented.	0
	Probably feasible: Some indication this can be implemented.	2
	Definitely feasible: Can be implemented.	5

Table 11. Internal Controls Key Performance Results Communication 3rd Round Data: Non-consensus.

Statement	Ratings	Total Number of Panelist Who Selected Each Ratings
Statement 45 – Internal control activities towards capital regulation that can be effective in reducing losses includes		

Table 11. *(Continued)*

Statement	Ratings	Total Number of Panelist Who Selected Each Ratings
communication to management key monthly performance results and risk assessments.		
	Highly undesirable: Will have major negative effect.	0
	Undesirable: Will have a negative effect with little or no positive effect.	2
	Neither desirable nor undesirable: Will have equal positive and negative effects.	1
	Desirable: Will have a positive effect with minimum negative effects.	4
	Highly desirable: Will have a positive effect and little or no negative effect.	5
	Definitely infeasible: Cannot be implemented (unworkable).	1
	Probably infeasible: Some indication this cannot be implemented.	1
	May or may not be feasible: Contradictory evidence this can be implemented.	0
	Probably feasible: Some indication this can be implemented.	2
	Definitely feasible: Can be implemented.	5

Table 12. Internal Controls Scope of Financial and Operational Control 3rd Round Data: Non-consensus.

Statement	Ratings	Total Number of Panelist Who Selected Each Ratings
Statement 47 – Internal control activities towards capital regulation that can be effective in reducing losses includes establishing scope of financial and operational controls.		
	Highly undesirable: Will have major negative effect.	0
	Undesirable: Will have a negative effect with little or no positive effect.	1
	Neither desirable nor undesirable: Will have equal positive and negative effects.	2
	Desirable: Will have a positive effect with minimum negative effects.	3
	Highly desirable: Will have a positive effect and little or no negative effect.	4
	Definitely infeasible: Cannot be implemented (unworkable).	2
	Probably infeasible: Some indication this cannot be implemented.	1
	May or may not be feasible: Contradictory evidence this can be implemented.	0
	Probably feasible: Some indication this can be implemented.	4
	Definitely feasible: Can be implemented.	3

Table 13. Internal Controls Risk Taxonomy 3rd Round Data: Consensus.

Statement	Ratings	Total Number of Panelist Who Selected Each Ratings
Statement 48 – Internal control activities towards capital regulation that can be effective in reducing losses includes having a Risk Taxonomy.		
	Highly undesirable: Will have major negative effect.	0
	Undesirable: Will have a negative effect with little or no positive effect.	1
	Neither desirable nor undesirable: Will have equal positive and negative effects.	1
	Desirable: Will have a positive effect with minimum negative effects	3
	Highly desirable: Will have a positive effect and little or no negative effect.	7
	Definitely infeasible: Cannot be implemented (unworkable).	0
	Probably infeasible: Some indication this cannot be implemented.	0
	May or may not be feasible: Contradictory evidence this can be implemented.	0
	Probably feasible: Some indication this can be implemented.	4
	Definitely feasible: Can be implemented.	4

Table 14. Internal Controls Monitoring of Account Activity 3rd Round Data: Non-consensus.

Statement	**Ratings**	**Total Number of Panelist Who Selected Each Ratings**
Statement 96 – Internal control activities towards capital regulation that can be effective in reducing losses includes continuous monitoring of account activity and to monitor the amount and type of activity for bank customers.		
	Highly undesirable: Will have major negative effect.	0
	Undesirable: Will have a negative effect with little or no positive effect.	1
	Neither desirable nor undesirable: Will have equal positive and negative effects.	3
	Desirable: Will have a positive effect with minimum negative effects.	4
	Highly desirable: Will have a positive effect and little or no negative effect.	3
	Definitely infeasible: Cannot be implemented (unworkable).	0
	Probably infeasible: Some indication this cannot be implemented.	0
	May or may not be feasible: Contradictory evidence this can be implemented.	2

Table 14. *(Continued)*

Statement	Ratings	Total Number of Panelist Who Selected Each Ratings
	Probably feasible: Some indication this can be implemented.	5
	Definitely feasible: Can be implemented.	3

Table 15. Internal Controls Monitoring Counterparty Credit Limit 3rd Round Data: Non-consensus.

Statement	Ratings	Total Number of Panelist Who Selected Each Ratings
Statement 125 – Internal control activities towards capital regulation that can be effective in reducing losses includes setting and monitoring counterparty credit limit.		
	Highly undesirable: Will have major negative effect.	0
	Undesirable: Will have a negative effect with little or no positive effect.	0
	Neither desirable nor undesirable: Will have equal positive and negative effects.	1
	Desirable: Will have a positive effect with minimum negative effects.	3

(Continued)

Table 15. *(Continued)*

Statement	Ratings	Total Number of Panelist Who Selected Each Ratings
	Highly desirable: Will have a positive effect and little or no negative effect.	4
	Definitely infeasible: Cannot be implemented (unworkable).	0
	Probably infeasible: Some indication this cannot be implemented.	1
	May or may not be feasible: Contradictory evidence this can be implemented.	1
	Probably feasible: Some indication this can be implemented.	5
	Definitely feasible: Can be implemented.	5

A good framework has various types of mitigation (risk assessment, control activities, information and communication, monitoring) activities (preventative, detective, monitoring) that are key controls and non-key that can help the organization meet its objectives in an effective manner. The use of internal controls in the United States has shown improvements in the quality of reporting and adherence to SOX in publicly traded companies (Hamed, 2023). The financial reports of publicly filed companies, along with SOX certifications from management, have provided investors/general consumers with financials they trust and information they have utilized to make purchasing or selling decisions. The lack of trustworthy information can have a direct impact on investor and consumer confidence in the markets. After the crises experience by Credit Suisse Bank and the collapse of Silicon Valley Bank, Swiss Bank marketers and service providers have faced many challenges and roadblocks in trying to maintain/receive consumer confidence and win back their trust (Suresh & Monalisa, 2024). This can have a negative economic and financial impact on the markets leading to significant losses. Baker et al. (2023) noted ICS and risk management used in banks are essential tools in facilitating their overarching success and assist these banks meet the objectives of shareholder value enhancement. The bank's board of directors have influence on the construction and monitoring of ICS; they ensures stakeholders and bank's objectives are met (Baker et al., 2023). An effective ICS assist banks and publicly filed companies in preventing bad financing, facilitate management to work in harmony in a structured control environment and assist in discovering errors and fraud in a timely manner (Baker et al., 2023).

The control framework should be constantly under review and updated to address changes in the industry (regulatory, accounting, geo-political, technology) and emerging risks. Banks and organizations should identify what can go wrong from being exposed to these constant changes and design mitigating measures to address these issues. Hamed (2023) stated economic, industry, regulatory and operational conditions face with changes that are constantly emerging; as such, it is imperative to implement systems and controls that can identify and mitigate associated risks with these changes. It is the obligation of administration to conduct performance, assessments, management, planning and identify controls to assist in the improvement and accomplishment of the organization's objectives (Baker et al., 2023). There is internal risk that arises from individuals within the company who have lack of knowledge of Securities and Exchange Commission (SEC) regulations and Generally Accepted Accounting Principles (GAAP) whose activities are not aligned to compliance requirements from these regulations (Hamed, 2023). This risk can cause deficiencies that leads to ineffective internal control practices (Hamed, 2023). The CEO and CFO are required to take ownership for certifying to the nature of the control environment and the financial statements as required by SOX (Act, 2002). Prior to SOX, this was not the requirement of the CEO and CFO; this ownership and attestation from senior management has contributed to an improved internal control environment.

Chapter 6

Challenges to the Effective Implementation of SOX Requirements

Many companies sent their lobbyists to Washington to kill the Sarbanes–Oxley (SOX) 2002 bill. These companies' complaints at first launch that the bill is over regulation of firms that were required to be compliant with Section 404(b) of the Act, which addresses reporting on company's internal controls (Coffee, 2018). The implementation and maintenance of SOX was a significant cost for small companies to become SOX compliant; this caused these companies to push back on the regulation, legislative actions, which led to cutbacks on some of the initial requirements of the bill (Coffee, 2018). Similarly, the subsequent measures put in place by the Fed after the 2008 financial crises address the root causes tied to weak internal controls faced challenges externally and internally. Congress authorizes a group of existing regulators to identify riskiest institutions and regulate them; institutions that engaged in systemically risky activities were warned they could be subjected to intensive oversight (Schwarcz & Zaring, 2017). Many corporations sent lobbyist to Washington to attack Fed measures to mitigate internal control weaknesses to prevent fraud and management misconduct. These measures were under-attacked and the possibility of being discontinued by lobbyist who went to Washington to block the Dodd–Frank Wall Street Reform and Consumer Protection Act of 2010 (Dodd–Frank Bill). Bank management would need to have internal control in place to ensure they meet the regulatory requirements in Dodd–Frank Bill. The Fed rolled out stricter capital regulations to both domestic and international banks that are subject to minimum capital adequacy and liquidity requirements (Wall, 2017). These regulations should focus on capital and financial system compliance at the systemic level that will improve the effective management of risk (Nitescu & Duna, 2016). Additionally, there is a call for more regulations of significant financial institutions that are interconnected financial system, nonbank financial institutions such as American International Group, Inc. that are a systemic risk (Wan, 2016).

Internal control activities designed to monitor capital through Basel III require a larger proportion of bank capital to be of high quality and conduct an annual stress test review completed (Wall, 2017). The Dodd–Frank Bill championed by

Effective Internal Control Practices in Banks, 81–92

doi:10.1108/978-1-83662-972-620251008

the Fed and consumers has been facing challenges form Lobbyist in Washington DC. Additionally, there were internal struggles within the Feds that place their major strides after the 2008 recession in regulating the banking sector, corporate governance of banks in the United States at the risk of being discontinued; the rules were challenged by many evils/dangers (Kim, 2016). The dangers were linked to internal power struggle from within the government agencies that led to deterioration of structures around Dodd–Frank Bill, corruption, cronyism and directed lending (Kim, 2016). There is the issue of funding that government agency has to overcome in order to be effective in carrying out their monitoring and enforcement role. The issuance of fines has provided regulatory agencies that were underfunded to receive increase in their budgets by keeping a percentage of the fines they issued (Prasch, 2012). Federal and state regulators issued indictment on fraudulent behaviours of management and impose fines and penalties (Prasch, 2012).

The Dodd–Frank Wall Street Reform and Consumer Protection Act of 2010 and it's Volcker Rule section faced roll out challenges, delays and the threats of being repealed in the United States (Trendowski & Rustambekov, 2017). Both the Dodd–Frank Bill and its subsection Volker rule set-out to ban proprietary trading by banks with federally insured deposits (Trendowski & Rustambekov, 2017). Dodd–Frank Act of 2010's aims and efforts were geared towards limiting risk-seeking behaviour; however, trades related to market-making were given an exemption if they met at least seven standards (Trendowski & Rustambekov, 2017). This global effort to curtail high-risk trading behaviour met challenges because many corporate leaders saw strong regulation as a negative impact in countries with poorly developed banking sectors; many thought the one-size-fits-all approach to good regulation is not feasible (Maxfield & Sousa, 2015). The efforts of government regulators to curtail weak control practices that led to collapse of public companies and banks have not been successful. If SOX was fully successful in 2002, the issues of weak internal controls that did not prevent management abuse and fraud would not have caused the 2008 recession. Many of the root causes lobbyist gave the regulators in Washington to repeal SOX was it causes loss of business opportunities.

Stigliano (2011) mentioned that after the SOX Law was passed, the financial markets experienced a significant loss of $1.4 trillion in shareholder wealth. Although the measure of SOX is beneficial to the investor/consumer investments and provides more credible information to utilize in their purchasing of stocks and other investments in the markets, the cost was seen by many to outweigh the benefit. The panel of expert's statements related to SOX that had low desirability and feasibility ratings from the panel of experts are noted below. These statements votes are displayed in Tables (16–18) (Velez, 2020).

Stigliano (2011) asserts Blackstone CEO argued that SOX is a good thing for his business, but the flip side is that it is the worst thing that happened to America. The subsequent events after the passing of SOX reflected that many corporations went from public to private to avoid the SOX because of the exuberant cost from implementation and maintenance of the Act (Stigliano, 2011). There is the issue of lawsuits filed against the Public Company Accounting Oversight Board

Table 16. Internal Controls Risk Controls Self-assessment 2nd Round Data: Non-consensus.

Statement	Ratings	Total Number of Panelist Who Selected Each Ratings
Statement 131 – Internal control activities towards capital regulation that can be effective in reducing losses includes performing frequent a scheduled risk control self assessments.		
	Highly undesirable: Will have major negative effect.	0
	Undesirable: Will have a negative effect with little or no positive effect.	0
	Neither desirable nor undesirable: Will have equal positive and negative effects.	2
	Desirable: Will have a positive effect with minimum negative effects.	2
	Highly desirable: Will have a positive effect and little or no negative effect.	2
	Probably infeasible: Some indication this cannot be implemented.	0
	May or may not be feasible: Contradictory evidence this can be implemented.	3
	Probably feasible: Some indication this can be implemented.	0
	Definitely feasible: Can be implemented.	5

Table 17. Internal Controls Change Management Programme 2nd Round Data: Non-consensus.

Statement	Ratings	Total Number of Panelist Who Selected Each Ratings
Statement 132 – Internal control activities towards capital regulation that can be effective in reducing losses includes implementing effective change management programme.		
	Highly undesirable: Will have major negative effect.	0
	Undesirable: Will have a negative effect with little or no positive effect.	0
	Neither desirable nor undesirable: Will have equal positive and negative effects.	2
	Desirable: Will have a positive effect with minimum negative effects.	2
	Highly desirable: Will have a positive effect and little or no negative effect.	2
	Definitely infeasible: Cannot be implemented (unworkable).	0
	Probably infeasible: Some indication this cannot be implemented.	0
	May or may not be feasible: Contradictory evidence this can be implemented.	1

Table 17. *(Continued)*

Statement	Ratings	Total Number of Panelist Who Selected Each Ratings
	Probably feasible: Some indication this can be implemented.	4
	Definitely feasible: Can be implemented.	4

Table 18. Internal Controls Strict Risk Management 3rd Round Data: Non-consensus.

Statement	Ratings	Total Number of Panelist Who Selected Each Ratings
Statement 21 – Internal control activities towards capital regulation that can be effective in reducing losses includes strict risk management.		
	Highly undesirable: Will have major negative effect.	0
	Undesirable: Will have a negative effect with little or no positive effect.	1
	Neither desirable nor undesirable: Will have equal positive and negative effects.	2
	Desirable: Will have a positive effect with minimum negative effects.	4
	Highly desirable: Will have a positive effect and little or no negative effect.	3

(Continued)

Table 18. *(Continued)*

Statement	Ratings	Total Number of Panelist Who Selected Each Ratings
	Definitely infeasible: Cannot be implemented (unworkable).	1
	Probably infeasible: Some indication this cannot be implemented.	1
	May or may not be feasible: Contradictory evidence this can be implemented.	3
	Probably feasible: Some indication this can be implemented.	3
	Definitely feasible: Can be implemented.	2

(PCAOB), a regulatory body charged with overseeing SOX audits completed by external auditors, who are one of the stakeholders of enforcement and monitoring of SOX. Title I of SOX creates the PCAOB or 'Board' to establish auditing standards that external audit firms (PWC, E&Y, KPMG) are required to plan, execute and prepare their audit reports; these audit firms workpapers used to examine the publicly filed companies are independently reviewed by the PCAOB (Thomsen & Norman, 2008). SOX Act Section 104 stipulated that the PCAOB should perform Board annual inspection of external audit firms that provide audit reports for more than 100 public companies and every three years if they perform fewer audits to ensure these firms are in compliance with SOX (Thomsen & Norman, 2008). Publicly traded company on a national exchange must file annually 10k audited financial statements that are in compliance with the Securities and Exchange Commission (the 'Commission' or SEC) regulations. The SEC mandate is to enforce the securities laws and regulations (Thomsen & Norman, 2008). The SEC requires publicly traded companies' senior management (CEOs, CFOs) who filed a financial statement with annual revenues of more than $1.2 billon to file sworn statements attesting to the accuracy of the financials pursuant to Section 21(a)(1) of the Securities Exchange Act of 1934 (Thomsen & Norman, 2008). However, the PCAOB role has been challenged by firms who filed lawsuit against the regulator. Many challenged the structure and appointment of the PCAOB that the SEC should not be appointing the PCAOB and its members to perform this role to oversee SOX. There was a lawsuit filed (Free Enterprise Fund v. Public Company Accounting Oversight Board) in 2006 challenging the SEC and not the President who appointed the PCAOB and its officers to regulate the accounting industry (Rao, 2010). There are other challenges stemming from weak implementation of the internal control system as predicated by SOX which makes the control activities ineffective in preventing and detecting an issue in a timely manner.

Bank management and internal stakeholder mindset towards internal controls is very weak. Shi and Wang's (2014) internal control consciousness in banks is weak, and they believe there are similarities between internal control accounting approach and audit supervision; this caused them to neglect business operation management and the role the accounting staff play in this process. There is a lack of strictness in internal control activities, failures to implement detailed rules for business implementation and rigorous standards (Shi & Wang, 2014). Internal control failures and business operating system failures in effective control around accounting processes and business are linked to system risk (Shi & Wang, 2014). One of the systems that supports internal control is the accounting information system that has faced challenges linked to its complex nature and design. Baker et al. (2023) posit banks' internal control process and system is difficult to master without leveraging a significant amount of information from the business. Managing a significant amount of data requires use of accounting information system (AIS) to obtain information needed in the control process (Baker et al., 2023). The role of internal control is a mechanism used to monitor, detect and prevent risk-driven bank activities (Baker et al., 2023). AIS is the source of financial data that impact banks' performance, and the effectiveness of the system is impacted by the complexity of the issues influencing the company's performance (Baker et al., 2023). Additionally, there are other actionable items namely decision-making process, quality of decisions, energetic bank employees, and efficiency and effectiveness that also have an impact on the system performance (Baker et, al, 2023). A measure tool that reflects the effectiveness and quality of AIS is noted in the nature of reporting which is directly aligned to the bank's success.

System risk can derail the effectiveness of internal control activities in meeting its designed goals and objectives. The bank developed electronic and network systems that lacked technical support which led to system breaches (Shi & Wang, 2014). The banks utilized automated controls as a mitigation measure to provide coverage of all business risks relating to the lack of automatic control that were manual in nature (Shi & Wang, 2014). The bank's rules and regulations were lagging behind regulatory requirements that companies relied on for the development of network technology to meet those compliance requirements (Shi & Wang, 2014). Alampalli (2013) posits regulatory data are on separate information systems which is a barrier to accessibility to the teams who need this information to make important decisions and prevents them from sharing this information with peers. The regulatory tools and data collection methods are not current and are unable to address regulatory changes in the financial system (Alampalli, 2013). Meager (2017) mentioned system developments are unable to meet banks' regulatory needs unless they serve a business purpose; this purpose can be the automation of mass administrative tasks, internal control requirement as specified by SOX.

Banks are required to report on their losses both in the audited financial statements and senior management attest to the effectiveness of controls activities which covers losses. Loss databases and systems have been found to be unreliable due to their design. Members of the expert panel see data management as doubtful exercises when they are not automated. Control activities relating to timely monthly/quarterly reporting, use of internal and external risk loss databases provided by Operational Risk Exchange (ORX) and change management in banks and public companies failed to meet the 60% consensus threshold. Goldberg (2017) mentioned there is an ecosystem of risks stemming from market data, databases, computer and non-automated systems which have significant impacts on calculations and business decisions. Old systems that have been used in business processing and reporting have become outdated in the enhanced regulatory environment. Shi and Wang (2014) noted banks original systems fail to meet the rapid expansion of business scope and regulatory requirements. Bank practices are unclear to new business partners and their internal controls practices are ineffective (Shi & Wang, 2014). Banks fail to establish a robust accounting internal control supervision and evaluation system; this caused transactions processed to be unsupervised and unrestricted (Shi & Wang, 2014). Banks should implement a strong technological infrastructure that will assist them in achieving data quality and availability to meet effective regulatory requirements (Boora & Kavita, 2018). Data management principles and requirements failed to meet the 60% consensus threshold for the panel of expert voted which supports the scepticism around data management and communication. These statements votes are displayed in Tables (19–21) (Velez, 2020).

Table 19. Internal Controls ORX Loss Database 2nd Round Data: Non-consensus.

Statement	**Ratings**	**Total Number of Panelist Who Selected Each Ratings**
Statement 14 – Internal control activities towards capital regulation that can be effective in reducing losses includes use of internal and external Operational Risk Exchange (ORX) loss databases to benchmark against industry.		

Table 19. *(Continued)*

Statement	Ratings	Total Number of Panelist Who Selected Each Ratings
	Highly undesirable: Will have major negative effect.	2
	Undesirable: Will have a negative effect with little or no positive effect.	0
	Neither desirable nor undesirable: Will have equal positive and negative effects.	3
	Highly desirable: Will have a positive effect and little or no negative effect.	2
	Definitely infeasible: Cannot be implemented (unworkable).	0
	Probably infeasible: Some indication this cannot be implemented.	1
	May or may not be feasible: Contradictory evidence this can be implemented.	0
	Probably feasible: Some indication this can be implemented.	6
	Definitely feasible: Can be implemented.	2

Banks lack a comprehensive analysis and evaluation of control issues root causes; they are unable to mitigate and remediate those control gaps and risks (Shi & Wang, 2014). Senior Management in banks who are tasked with overseeing and monitoring the control environment ignore the urgency of addressing control issues/gaps identified. Shi and Wang (2014) noted banks have ignored the test evaluation results of SOX internal control which caused them to miss real-time

Table 20. Change Controls Alignment With Technology Governance 2nd Round Data: Non-consensus.

Statement	Ratings	Total Number of Panelist Who Selected Each Ratings
Statement 29 – Governance practices senior bank managers can implement towards capital regulation that are effective in reducing losses entails change controls alignment with technology governance.		
	Highly undesirable: Will have major negative effect.	0
	Undesirable: Will have a negative effect with little or no positive effect.	1
	Neither desirable nor undesirable: Will have equal positive and negative effects.	1
	Desirable: Will have a positive effect with minimum negative effects.	2
	Highly desirable: Will have a positive effect and little or no negative effect.	3
	Definitely infeasible: Cannot be implemented (unworkable).	0
	Probably infeasible: Some indication this cannot be implemented.	0
	May or may not be feasible: Contradictory evidence this can be implemented.	3

Table 20. *(Continued)*

Statement	Ratings	Total Number of Panelist Who Selected Each Ratings
	Probably feasible: Some indication this can be implemented.	2
	Definitely feasible: Can be implemented.	5

Table 21. Internal Controls UIPath Robot Processing 2nd Round Data: Non-consensus.

Statement	Ratings	Total Number of Panelist Who Selected Each Ratings
Statement 110 – Internal control activities towards capital regulation that can be effective in reducing losses includes use of UIPath Robot processing is one area of automation that is a viable option.		
	Highly undesirable: Will have major negative effect.	0
	Undesirable: Will have a negative effect with little or no positive effect.	0
	Neither desirable nor undesirable: Will have equal positive and negative effects.	3
	Desirable: Will have a positive effect with minimum negative effects.	1

(Continued)

Table 21. *(Continued)*

Statement	**Ratings**	**Total Number of Panelist Who Selected Each Ratings**
	Highly desirable: Will have a positive effect and little or no negative effect.	1
	Definitely infeasible: Cannot be implemented (unworkable).	1
	Probably infeasible: Some indication this cannot be implemented.	0
	May or may not be feasible: Contradictory evidence this can be implemented.	2
	Probably feasible: Some indication this can be implemented.	3
	Definitely feasible: Can be implemented.	2

monitoring and timely warning. This lack of paying attention to internal control test results has prevented management from improving the effectiveness of the internal control system (Shi & Wang, 2014).

Chapter 7

Regulators, Auditors and Process Owners Failures in SOX Certification Process

Sarbanes Oxley Act 2002 (SOX) regulation has 11 sections which outline requirements that regulators (PCAOB), auditors (EY, PWC, Audit Firms) and process owners/senior management (CEO, CFO) should comply with annually/tri-annually. Many of these stakeholders faced challenges and failures in executing these guidelines resulting in them having to pay penalties and findings for non-compliance. External audit firms are required to perform an audit of the public company financial report and internal controls. One finding brought against Ernst and Young (EY) is their failure to challenge or question the missing disclosure of a $50 billion debt of a company they audited (Thomsen & Norman, 2008). EY was sued by Andrew M. Cuomo (New York Attorney General) in December of 2010 for its role in helping Lehman Brothers commit accounting Fraud (Thomsen & Norman, 2008). Lehman Brothers deceived investors in presenting the bank's financial health as one that is sound which was a significant financial fraud and falsification of financial information; the company filed shortly thereafter bankruptcy and their senior managements were told y had gross inaccuracies in their financial statements (Thomsen & Norman, 2008). Lehman used Repo, a window-dressing tool to make the bank appear to be more liquid and financially healthy, lowered their risk, while their debt and financial leverage grew bigger each quarter (Stigliano, 2011). The last quarter of 2007 Lehman debt was $39 billion, first quarter of 2008 it grew to $49 billion, and second quarter of 2008 the debt was $50 billion (Stigliano, 2011). Shortly after in 2008, JPMorgan and Citigroup called Lehman requested that Lehman pay back their borrowed money which led to Leman filing for bankruptcy in September of 2008 (Stigliano, 2011). Eliot Spitzer, former NY Governor, argued that Lehman's primary motive behind these types of weird sale transactions was to defraud the market (Stigliano, 2011). Despite this factor of significant inaccuracies in Lehman Brothers financials, EY did not take preventative measures and the respective due diligence to prevent further damage; this was seen as EY grossly disregarding the law and a clear act of them breaking the law (Thomsen & Norman, 2008). Richard Fuld Lehman CEO paid himself $500 million over 15 years using the illegal

Effective Internal Control Practices in Banks, 93–103

Published under exclusive licence by Emerald Publishing Limited
doi:10.1108/978-1-83662-972-620251009

transactions of Repo that was never questioned or challenged by Ernst and Young regarding missing disclosure of the $50 billion debt (Stigliano, 2011). Similarly, KPMG LLP in 2005 admitted to criminal wrongdoing and paid $456 million in fines as part of an agreement to stop prosecution of the firm (Stigliano, 2011).

What about the audit board that appointed EY and the company's board of directors who both received the audited financials? Did they too fail to question the quality and accuracy of audited financials of Lehman Brothers? Hideaki and Naoki (2021) assert large public companies must appoint external auditors, such as EY accounting auditors that are approved by the audit board; these auditors perform a financial statement audit/assurance and attestation services of the firms activities and submit the financial reports to both the board of directors and the audit board. The members of the audit board have the right to challenge, question, audit the reporting process and results and to express their opinions of the financial reports (Hideaki & Naoki, 2021). There were many stakeholders and consumers who questioned what can go wrong that went overlooked by many who were commissioned to monitor the activities and financial health of Lehman Brothers. One of the senior vice presidents overseeing Lehman's global balance sheet posed questions to EY and challenged the audit firm's professional expertise to properly perform the audit functions they were engaged to perform (Thomsen & Norman, 2008). There is the issue of rotational system where personnel failed to implement systems of rotation; this has led to long-term accumulated irregularities, detection risk and timely remediation activities which perpetuate bank risk (Shi & Wang, 2014). There are assurance practices that failed to meet the 60% consensus threshold for the panel of experts. These statement votes are displayed in Tables (22–27) (Velez, 2020).

Table 22. Assurance Practices Monitoring of All Balance Sheet Activity 2nd Round Data: Non-consensus.

Statement	Ratings	Total Number of Panelist Who Selected Each Ratings
Statement 97 – Assurance practices towards capital regulation that can be effective in reducing losses incudes continuous monitoring of all balance sheet activity.		
	Highly undesirable: Will have major negative effect.	0

Table 22. *(Continued)*

Statement	Ratings	Total Number of Panelist Who Selected Each Ratings
	Undesirable: Will have a negative effect with little or no positive effect.	1
	Neither desirable nor undesirable: Will have equal positive and negative effects.	1
	Desirable: Will have a positive effect with minimum negative effects.	2
	Highly desirable: Will have a positive effect and little or no negative effect.	2
	Definitely infeasible: Cannot be implemented (unworkable).	0
	Probably infeasible: Some indication this cannot be implemented.	0
	May or may not be feasible: Contradictory evidence this can be implemented.	3
	Probably feasible: Some indication this can be implemented.	2
	Definitely feasible: Can be implemented.	4

It was echoed by Shi and Wang (2014) banks have several problems which includes but not limited to the lack of initiative in accounting supervisor, lack of professional ethics consciousness, sense of responsibility and insufficient standard operation behaviour. Additionally, Sarbanes Oxley (Section 404) required CEO and CFO (higher-up management) to certify the published financial statements

Table 23. Assurance Practices Managed Within Regulatory Guidelines 3rd Round Data: Non-consensus.

Statement	Ratings	Total Number of Panelist Who Selected Each Ratings
Statement 15 – Assurance practices towards capital regulation that can be effective in reducing losses incudes tools available to them to ensure that capital regulation are managed to within guidelines established by regulatory authorities.		
	Highly undesirable: Will have major negative effect.	1
	Undesirable: Will have a negative effect with little or no positive effect.	2
	Neither desirable nor undesirable: Will have equal positive and negative effects.	1
	Desirable: Will have a positive effect with minimum negative effects.	2
	Highly desirable: Will have a positive effect and little or no negative effect.	1
	Definitely infeasible: Cannot be implemented (unworkable).	1
	Probably infeasible: Some indication this cannot be implemented.	0
	May or may not be feasible: Contradictory evidence this can be implemented.	1

Table 23. *(Continued)*

Statement	Ratings	Total Number of Panelist Who Selected Each Ratings
	Probably feasible: Some indication this can be implemented.	6
	Definitely feasible: Can be implemented.	3

Table 24. Assurance Practices Quality Analysis Metrics 3rd Round Data: Non-consensus.

Statement	Ratings	Total Number of Panelist Who Selected Each Ratings
Statement 52 – Assurance practices towards capital regulation that can be effective in reducing losses incudes on-going quality assurance analysis with metrics (score card/dash board).		
	Highly undesirable: Will have major negative effect.	0
	Undesirable: Will have a negative effect with little or no positive effect.	1
	Neither desirable nor undesirable: Will have equal positive and negative effects.	4
	Desirable: Will have a positive effect with minimum negative effects.	3

(Continued)

Table 24. *(Continued)*

Statement	Ratings	Total Number of Panelist Who Selected Each Ratings
	Highly desirable: Will have a positive effect and little or no negative effect.	4
	Definitely infeasible: Cannot be implemented (unworkable).	0
	Probably infeasible: Some indication this cannot be implemented.	0
	May or may not be feasible: Contradictory evidence this can be implemented.	1
	Probably feasible: Some indication this can be implemented.	6
	Definitely feasible: Can be implemented.	1

Table 25. Assurance Practices Independent Quality Assurance Process 3rd Round Data: Non-consensus.

Statement	Ratings	Total Number of Panelist Who Selected Each Ratings
Statement 53 – Assurance practices towards capital regulation that can be effective in reducing losses incudes establishment of an independent quality assurance process with best practices expectations.		

Table 25. *(Continued)*

Statement	Ratings	Total Number of Panelist Who Selected Each Ratings
	Highly undesirable: Will have major negative effect.	0
	Undesirable: Will have a negative effect with little or no positive effect.	1
	Neither desirable nor undesirable: Will have equal positive and negative effects.	3
	Desirable: Will have a positive effect with minimum negative effects.	5
	Highly desirable: Will have a positive effect and little or no negative effect.	3
	Definitely infeasible: Cannot be implemented (unworkable).	0
	Probably infeasible: Some indication this cannot be implemented.	1
	May or may not be feasible: Contradictory evidence this can be implemented.	1
	Probably feasible: Some indication this can be implemented.	4
	Definitely feasible: Can be implemented.	2

comply with Securities and Exchange Commission standards which was a failed control activity (Thomsen & Norman, 2008). The CEO and CFO of Lehman Brothers both did not execute the control activities that challenge and review

Table 26. Assurance Practices Evaluation Standards and Monitoring 3rd Round Data: Non-consensus.

Statement	**Ratings**	**Total Number of Panelist Who Selected Each Ratings**
Statement 54 – Assurance practices towards capital regulation that can be effective in reducing losses incudes evaluation standards and monitoring.		
	Highly undesirable: Will have major negative effect.	0
	Undesirable: Will have a negative effect with little or no positive effect.	2
	Neither desirable nor undesirable: Will have equal positive and negative effects.	1
	Desirable: Will have a positive effect with minimum negative effects.	4
	Highly desirable: Will have a positive effect and little or no negative effect.	4
	Definitely infeasible: Cannot be implemented (unworkable).	1
	Probably infeasible: Some indication this cannot be implemented.	0
	May or may not be feasible: Contradictory evidence this can be implemented.	1
	Probably feasible: Some indication this can be implemented.	4
	Definitely feasible: Can be implemented.	3

Table 27. Assurance Practices Proactive Address Credit Risk Problems 3rd Round Data: Non-consensus.

Statement	**Ratings**	**Total Number of Panelist Who Selected Each Ratings**
Statement 74 – Assurance practices towards capital regulation that can be effective in reducing losses incudes banks being proactive in addressing potential credit risk problems.		
	Highly undesirable: Will have major negative effect.	0
	Undesirable: Will have a negative effect with little or no positive effect.	0
	Neither desirable nor undesirable: Will have equal positive and negative effects.	1
	Desirable: Will have a positive effect with minimum negative effects.	4
	Highly desirable: Will have a positive effect and little or no negative effect.	5
	Definitely infeasible: Cannot be implemented (unworkable).	1
	Probably infeasible: Some indication this cannot be implemented.	1
	May or may not be feasible: Contradictory evidence this can be implemented.	0

(Continued)

Table 27. *(Continued)*

Statement	Ratings	Total Number of Panelist Who Selected Each Ratings
	Probably feasible: Some indication this can be implemented.	4
	Definitely feasible: Can be implemented.	4

financial and operational activities that is linked to the financial statements. Their assertions to the financial soundness of the financial reports were grossly reckless and inaccurate. There are different levels of stakeholders who should have prevented the financial fraud issue at Lehman Brothers, but all levels of preventative controls stakeholder of SOX failed. The CEO, CFO and senior management of the organization must attest to their methodology used to establish and maintain an adequate internal control structure and procedures for financial reporting (Thomsen & Norman, 2008). The senior management of the bank is charged with overseeing the accounting information system which aims to provide reliability in operation, accurate, trustworthy information to its users and timely financial information (Baker et al., 2023). However, Stigliano (2011) mentioned forensic accountants poses concerning fact that the Section 404 sign-off within the SOX act by the CEO and CFO to soundness of SOX in their organization is nothing but a check the box; Forensic personnel stated 84% of the frauds over the past 10 years involved the CEO and/or CFO. Having the CEO and CFO sign a Section 404 certification had little impact on decreasing fraud levels and financial statement restatements (Stigliano, 2011).

The integrity of the financial information, resources of the bank, relies on having acceptable internal control in place, and to achieve this objective, the bank must prioritize both system and employee issues as part of the framework (Baker et al., 2023).The next level of failure of control activities that PCAOB mandated EY as external auditors to perform which failed to prevent financial misstatements and inaccuracies in the financial results; why was Ernst & Young's professional scepticism not applied in this audit to prevent the misrepresentation of the financial results of Lehman Brothers? (Thomsen & Norman, 2008). Additionally, the SEC who review the filed financial statements quarterly and annually as per the Securities law and the requirements of Sarbanes–Oxley trusted to the SEC failed to detect this scandal timely and prevented the damage to the financial markets (Thomsen & Norman, 2008). Besides the issue of Lehman Brothers failures and inaccuracies of the audited financials that he public relies on to make inform decision, there was the issue of HealthSouth Corporation. An investigation was launched into HealthSouth September 2002 shortly after SOX 2002 Act was placed into law; It was noted that HealthSouth executives committed accounting fraud and overstated earnings by $1.4 billion which began in 1999 (Thomsen & Norman, 2008). The SEC charged two former HealthSouth executives with insider trading, securities fraud and false certification of financial records; HealthSouth executives fraudulently represented $2.5 billion in earnings (Thomsen & Norman, 2008). Al-Matari et al. (2017) assert that the board of directors tend to keep their knowledge of the company's distorted financial statement a secret as they lacked independence from senior management. Again, the auditors of Ernst & Young admitted that they relied on a handful of people for information about how HealthSouth was managed and did not properly check and test certain account balances (Thomsen & Norman, 2008). HealthSouth case scandal caught was brought to public forefront because SOX and US officials asserted enactment of SOX will lead to corporate-fraud prosecutions, intensify scandals are identified in effective and efficient time (Thomsen & Norman, 2008). The Federal Bureau of Investigation (FBI), Department of Justice (DOJ), local US attorneys and SEC worked as a team to prosecute executives involved in corporate fraud (Thomsen & Norman, 2008).

Chapter 8

Internal Control Framework (Preventive, Detective, Monitoring, Automated) Design

Banks have to rely on designing an effective internal control system to achieve its goal of fairness and accuracy in the financial reporting process (Hideaki & Naoki, 2021). Control environment helps to attain internal control system goals and improvement of system quality of the organization through the discipline and structure of the environment in which it thrives, thereby impacting operational effectiveness (Frank et al., 2023). Securities and Exchange Commission (SEC) requires banks and publicly filed companies to attest to effectiveness of their internal controls and the state of their overall control environment as required by Sarbanes–Oxley Act in 2002 Section 404(b). Sarbanes–Oxley Act in 2002 Section 404 requires a report on the adequacy of the company's internal control environment which should be audited by an external audit firm (Coffee, 2018). The public company's internal controls focus is on the accuracy of its financial statements, exposure to fraud and misappropriation while overlooking the financial institution's exposure to risk (Coffee, 2018). As such, the design of the control environment should consist of structures, methods and measures that are foundational in the evaluation of the internal control framework (Frank et al., 2023). The framework/design of internal controls system should include foundational pieces such as control environment, risk assessment, control activities, information and communication and monitoring (Al-Hawatmeh, 2021). Internal control activities design and operating effectiveness are relevant to maintain a sustainable system with a mixture of manual and automated.

Many banks' control environment is either passive or active. An active and positive control environment displays proactive responsiveness, actionable rules and standards, receptive to change without interruption of daily system's structure and functional activeness (Helena & Madsen, 2021). All stakeholders of the control environment work together for the well-being of the corporation and to achieve and maintain a proactive compliance environment (Helena & Madsen, 2021). This inclusive approach incorporates all lines of defence as Ghosh (2021) mentioned the various lines of defenses involved in the monitoring of the environment in the bank includes: (i) first line of defence that are business level

Effective Internal Control Practices in Banks, 105–113

Published under exclusive licence by Emerald Publishing Limited
doi:10.1108/978-1-83662-972-620251010

executives/managing directors (create policies and procedures, personnel communication); (ii) second line of defence Chief Risk Officer (monitoring of AML/CFT policies) independent of business line responsibilities; (iii) third line of defence – internal audit (audit banks activities and report to audit committee). The collaboration of the various line of defence in a proactive manner facilitates a control environment that is low risk in nature; the inverse of no collaboration among these stakeholders would be a high-risk control environment. The control environment is the attitude, style and philosophy of the stakeholders (Board of Directors, Senior Management, CEO, CFO employees of the company) that are interconnected with the organization which is evidenced in measurable activities that display their competency, morale, integrity and ethical values (Frank et al., 2023). Bank management dedication to ethical business practices is demonstrated in the control environment which sets the tone of the organization and enhances employee behaviour and organizational performance (Frank et al., 2023). As such, internal control systems which live within the control environment must be incorporated into the company's operational activities to detect, prevent misstatements and provide assurance in meeting performance targets (Frank et al., 2023). In building the control environment, risk identification is critical to identify internal factors (institutional account structure, corresponding contracts, nature of institutional activities, institution's human resources quality, organizational changes, employee turnover) and external factors (industry changes, technological advances), which contributes to a high-risk environment and the type of control activities needed to prevent, detect and monitor these activities and normalize the control environment (Izhar & Asutay, 2010).

The Enterprise-Wide Risk Assessment (EWRA) methodology identifies possible risks faced by the firm, and it is approved by the board of directors; this adds credibility and lessened biases in assessment results (Duncan, 2021). The EWRA methodology approved by the Board communicate purpose and direction of the bank set the risk appetite, tolerable bank risk, measurement approach and risk treatments within and outside the tolerable limits (Duncan, 2021). The EWRA programme identifies, assesses and manages potential roadblocks and takes mitigation measures to minimize these risks with the help of the stakeholders (Duncan, 2021). Risk rating measures and methodology should be carefully thought through and incorporated in the framework to gain efficiencies which includes risk identifications based on customer/business types and locations. The identification of risk based on customers (personal/business, local/foreign residents, low/medium/high-risk rating, business types, licenced and registered businesses, designated non-financial businesses, financial institutions) and the countries these business function in should be taken into consideration in the risk assessment process (Duncan, 2021). In order to sustain an effective EWRA programme, there should be a formalized policy and procedure that is actively enforced, clarity in record keeping, assessment and revising what processes work best as manual vs automation, computer-based systems, availability of reports, control officers, company-wide employee training, local laws compliance, regulations and guidance (Duncan, 2021). There should be the practice of scrutiny when reviewing business transactions (Duncan, 2021). Scrutiny and independent review are essential in identifying potential fraud in scenarios where there is internal collusion of internal staff and their deceptive activities to override bank controls and commit fraud with outside actors (Abiola & Oyewole, 2013). Collusion has been noted to render the banks control environment volatile to fraudulent activities that have caused banks significant losses, reputational damage, countless lawsuits and regulatory fines (Abiola & Oyewole, 2013).

Bank management in the establishment of control activities to mitigate identified risk within the organization should consider operations, specific characteristics of the organization and the control environment. The principles of the control environment should demonstrate management dedication to ethical business practices; management with ethical principles displays these principles in their day-to-day execution of business activities that influence employee behavior and organization performance. Internal control activities are designed to play the role of detective, preventative, directive, corrective or compensatory or monitoring. These functions are aimed to decrease substantial errors, omissions, wastes, purposeful acts and fraudulent transactions which impact negatively on a company's performance (Frank et al., 2023). Banks use review and approvals by supervisors, managers and directors who are separate from the preparers of these control activities to prevent errors and fraudulent acts by employees which are sometimes ineffective due to collusion. This weakness in the process can be related to poorly documented procedures that are poorly communicated and accessible in the company and failure to apply procedures that do exist into practice (Hemrit & Arab, 2013). There is a lack of trained employees and shortage of individuals with the skill set to perform the respective business transactions per the required guidelines; the skill shortages and lack of awareness to the details of the process which cause errors in financial reports (Hemrit & Arab, 2013). This error may go undetected because of the lack of skills and knowledge of the subject matter, actions such as fraud and embezzlement that can cause immense losses (Hemrit & Arab, 2013). There are effective control activities that are designed to mitigate risks within the control environment that the panel of experts reached consensus. These statement votes are displayed in Tables (28–31) (Velez, 2020).

Table 28. Internal Control Activities That Include Three Lines of Defence 3rd Round Data: Consensus.

Statement	**Ratings**	**Total Number of Panelist Who Selected Each Ratings**
Statement 46 – Internal control activities towards capital regulation that can be effective in reducing		

(Continued)

Table 28. *(Continued)*

Statement	Ratings	Total Number of Panelist Who Selected Each Ratings
losses includes use of three lines of defence adopting division policies as needed.		
	Highly undesirable: Will have major negative effect.	0
	Undesirable: Will have a negative effect with little or no positive effect.	2
	Neither desirable nor undesirable: Will have equal positive and negative effects.	6
	Desirable: Will have a positive effect with minimum negative effects.	2
	Highly desirable: Will have a positive effect and little or no negative effect.	2
	Definitely infeasible: Cannot be implemented (unworkable).	0
	Probably infeasible: Some indication this cannot be implemented.	0
	May or may not be feasible: Contradictory evidence this can be implemented.	2
	Probably feasible: Some indication this can be implemented.	4
	Definitely feasible: Can be implemented.	2

Table 29. Internal Control Activities That Include Risk Taxonomy 3rd Round Data: Consensus.

Statement	Ratings	Total Number of Panelist Who Selected Each Ratings
Statement 48 – Internal control activities towards capital regulation that can be effective in reducing losses includes having a risk taxonomy.		
	Highly undesirable: Will have major negative effect.	0
	Undesirable: Will have a negative effect with little or no positive effect.	1
	Neither desirable nor undesirable: Will have equal positive and negative effects.	1
	Desirable: Will have a positive effect with minimum negative effects.	3
	Highly desirable: Will have a positive effect and little or no negative effect.	7
	Definitely infeasible: Cannot be implemented (unworkable).	0
	Probably infeasible: Some indication this cannot be implemented.	0
	May or may not be feasible: Contradictory evidence this can be implemented.	0
	Probably feasible: Some indication this can be implemented.	4
	Definitely feasible: Can be implemented.	4

Table 30. Internal Control Activities That Include Employee Follow Procedures 3rd Round Data: Consensus.

Statement	Ratings	Total Number of Panelist Who Selected Each Ratings
Statement 86 – Internal control activities towards capital regulation that can be effective in reducing losses includes ensuring employees have time to recognise problems and follow procedures and won't cut corners when they are not always under extreme pressure.		
	Highly undesirable: Will have major negative effect.	1
	Undesirable: Will have a negative effect with little or no positive effect.	2
	Neither desirable nor undesirable: Will have equal positive and negative effects.	0
	Desirable: Will have a positive effect with minimum negative effects.	1
	Highly desirable: Will have a positive effect and little or no negative effect.	6
	Definitely infeasible: Cannot be implemented (unworkable).	1
	Probably infeasible: Some indication this cannot be implemented.	2
	May or may not be feasible: Contradictory evidence this can be implemented.	3

Table 30. *(Continued)*

Statement	Ratings	Total Number of Panelist Who Selected Each Ratings
	Probably feasible: Some indication this can be implemented.	2
	Definitely feasible: Can be implemented.	2

Table 31. Internal Control Activities That Include Training Being a Priority 3rd Round Data: Consensus.

Statement	Ratings	Total Number of Panelist Who Selected Each Ratings
Statement 84 – Internal control activities towards capital regulation that can be effective in reducing losses includes making training a priority.		
	Highly undesirable: Will have major negative effect.	0
	Undesirable: Will have a negative effect with little or no positive effect.	0
	Neither desirable nor undesirable: Will have equal positive and negative effects.	0
	Desirable: Will have a positive effect with minimum negative effects.	3
	Highly desirable: Will have a positive effect and little or no negative effect.	6

(Continued)

Table 31. *(Continued)*

Statement	Ratings	Total Number of Panelist Who Selected Each Ratings
	Definitely infeasible: Cannot be implemented (unworkable).	1
	Probably infeasible: Some indication this cannot be implemented.	0
	May or may not be feasible: Contradictory evidence this can be implemented.	1
	Probably feasible: Some indication this can be implemented.	4
	Definitely feasible: Can be implemented.	5

There are other scenarios of collusion/overriding control activities in the control environment where controls sometimes are circumvented by employee's collusion with the supervisor assistance in overriding the controls. Hence some of these controls have been ineffective in preventing significant errors and internal fraud. Rogue trading is an operational risk event that is commonly blamed on inadequate supervision, collusion, override of controls that allows the rogue trader to break the rules (Schenk, 2017). Control environment can contribute to the growth or reduction losses as noted by Fadun and Oye (2020); the lack of effective internal control in Société Générale in 2008 resulted in USD 7.2 billion at Société Générale in losses. Similarly, the failure of control activities to prevent unauthorized transaction at Irish Allied Irisk Bank (AIB) led to $700 mn losses in the foreign exchange market in 2001, and Republic New York Corporation customer fraud resulted in a loss of $611 million (Anouar et al., 2017). To prevent risks that resulted in significant losses, it is necessary for banks to know the root cause of the risk event which helps them to understand and control this risk. Institutions implement fraud detection systems to mitigate fraudulent acts carried out independently by external third parties (de Jongh et al., 2013).

Information and communication are key to sharing results of information relating to identification, of risk captured, exchange of financial and operational information and requirements to be in compliance should be done in a timely manner; the communication of monitoring results of the quality of the internal control activities that has identified breakdown in the control systems in a timely manner (Abiola & Oyewole, 2013). Information and communication encompasses identification, processing and communicating information to all stakeholders at all levels (upward, downward) the bank; this ensures individuals at all levels are informed about various changes and developments (Chowdhury, 2021). The information shared through the control activities practiced in information and communication system validates the authenticity of the information, reliability and dissemination in a timely manner to make appropriate decisions (Chowdhury, 2021). Information and communication risk was evident in the use of wrong wording in financial protection products, payment protection insurance legal documents which caused losses of £264 million in payouts to customers in 2011 by UK banks (de Jongh et al., 2013). Banks use review and approvals by supervisors to prevent errors and fraudulent acts by employees which are sometimes ineffective internal control activities. This weakness in the process can be attributable to poorly documented procedures that have not been properly socialized throughout the company and/or failure to apply procedures that do exist (Hemrit & Arab, 2013). There are skills shortages, lack of consciousness, failure to pay attention to the details of the process resulting in errors in financial reports that go undetected; there are intentional fraud and embezzlement actions that can cause immense losses (Hemrit & Arab, 2013). There are other scenarios in the control environment where controls sometimes are circumvented by employees and the supervisor overriding the controls. Hence some of these controls have been ineffective in preventing significant errors and internal fraud such as rogue trading linked to inadequate supervision; this allows the rogue trader to break the rules (Schenk, 2017). Ferreira and Dickason-Koekemoer (2019) argue that banks failed controls led to significant losses have caused their own demise and other financial institutions. A successful internal control system ensures a complementary relationship, cooperative and periodic meetings between all stakeholders, namely the supervisory authority (Fed, SEC) and the internal and external auditors (Repousis et al., 2019). Monitoring activities are relevant to ensure effective performance of internal control, conformation regulatory requirements are met and reliance on operational and reporting activities (Chowdhury, 2021). Teams that are part of the monitoring process of risk in the control environment are mandated to report issues and develop recommendations; they should be proactive in identifying new trend dissemination that can be a threat to the business, assess risks and report the outcomes to stakeholders (Duncan, 2021).

Part 3

Bank Leadership Consensus on Designing Effective Control Environment

Chapter 9

Systems and the Automated Control Environment

A well-designed internal control environment should seek to automate many of its control activities and processes. The less manual reliance a process is in its operation, the lower the risk of errors and fraud. Shi and Wang (2014) noted bank systems need to have effective controls around its accounting business; the lack of system controls will contribute to system risk. The regulatory requirements proposed by the SEC, SOX and Feds have caused a drastic technological change in global markets to meet the new regulatory requirements and maintain their compliance standing. Many banks received findings for lack of compliance with the new regulatory changes. Banks face challenges with complying with new and amended regulations, meeting reporting guidelines within the time constraints posed by the regulators; automation of processes allows banks to obtain reliable data timely, reduce manual intervention and errors, while meeting the regulatory filing deadlines in a timely manner (Lai, 2018). Late filing for public companies and banks can expose the company to late fees and penalties, reduction in stock price and potential reputational damage. Banks should strive to achieve automation of processes which is beneficial to risk identification, improve data quality and readiness, meet regulatory reporting requirements and filings (Arner et al., 2017). Automation of processes allow global banks and the respective regulators to monitor and analyze real-time financial information available in many different countries in centralized, decentralized or shared services settings through linked systems. Meager (2017) mentioned technological benefits can be harnessed by banks to reduce cost burdens, while meeting regulatory compliance requirements. As such, system developments should be used by banks for the automation of mass administrative tasks imposed by the regulatory environment (Meager, 2017). Many organizations are seeking solutions through the implementation of IT-based solutions.

Banks are in the process of deploying accounting information systems (AIS) which is an IT-based solution that assists in the control of the company's financial and economic operations through its automation capabilities (Baker et al., 2023). The technological advancement of the AIS system will allow banks to a create accounting data in an environment where internal control system makes it easier

Effective Internal Control Practices in Banks, 117–126

doi:10.1108/978-1-83662-972-620251012

to operate (Baker et al., 2023). AIS has several methods and processes that make internal control system operations function effectively through simplifying the bank's operations, allowing the company to gain a competitive edge, and executing it processes/procedures with less mistakes (Baker et al., 2023). Furthermore, automation of data through systems can reduce ecosystem's risk as noted by Goldberg (2017) which stems from market data, databases, computer, nonautomated systems, inaccuracies in assumptions and calculations, developers, humans and computer programs. This data automation can assist in the global initiative of bank to accurately analyze internal and external risk loss data provided by Operational Risk Exchange (ORX) used to analyze performance individually vs industry benchmarks. This information equips banks to monitor bank assets and heighten awareness of risk factors. However, there are situations where technology if not properly used to meet regulatory requirements can result in inaccurate predictions based on systems problems. For example, banks have been using models to estimate losses and capital performance predictions which have inaccuracies. Banks are requirement to monitor their capital ratio, perform Risk Weighted Assets (RWA) and stress testing of capital calculations using the federal regulators risk models which have been ineffective (Dowd & Hutchinson, 2016). The panel of experts did not vote favourably towards the current state of ORX databases, Models used for Scenario Analysis and ineffective tools deployed by banks. These non-consensus statements votes are displayed in Tables (32–34) (Velez, 2020).

Table 32. Internal Control Activities ORX Loss Databases 2nd Round Data: Non-consensus.

Statement	Ratings	Total Number of Panelist Who Selected Each Ratings
Statement 14 – Internal control activities towards capital regulation that can be effective in reducing losses includes use of internal and external Operational Risk Exchange (ORX) loss databases to benchmark against industry.		
	Highly undesirable: Will have major negative effect.	2

Table 32. *(Continued)*

Statement	Ratings	Total Number of Panelist Who Selected Each Ratings
	Undesirable: Will have a negative effect with little or no positive effect.	0
	Neither desirable nor undesirable: Will have equal positive and negative effects.	3
	Highly desirable: Will have a positive effect and little or no negative effect.	2
	Definitely infeasible: Cannot be implemented (unworkable).	0
	Probably infeasible: Some indication this cannot be implemented.	1
	May or may not be feasible: Contradictory evidence this can be implemented.	0
	Probably feasible: Some indication this can be implemented.	6
	Definitely feasible: Can be implemented.	2

Fukuda (2016) asserts there is difficulty in financial tools used for model that is used to analyze the relationship between the financial conditions of financial intermediaries and the business cycle predictions. Similarly, Bellof and Wehn (2018) noted that models used in scenario analysis in banks lack data transparency, estimation errors, parameter uncertainties caused by algorithmic methods use of statistics, computational estimators' errors. The regulators require banks to perform capital stress testing using these models and run projections(revenue, income/losses, balance sheet assets, liabilities, capital ratios) and monitor these results in a continuous manner to ensure they are in

Table 33. Governance Practices Stress Tests on Vulnerable Areas 3rd Round Data: Non-consensus.

Statement	Ratings	Total Number of Panelist Who Selected Each Ratings
Statement 27 – Governance practices senior bank managers can implement towards capital regulation that are effective in reducing losses entails introduction of stress tests on vulnerable areas and assessment of the appropriateness of stress scenarios considered.		
	Highly undesirable: Will have major negative effect.	0
	Undesirable: Will have a negative effect with little or no positive effect.	1
	Neither desirable nor undesirable: Will have equal positive and negative effects.	1
	Desirable: Will have a positive effect with minimum negative effects.	4
	Highly desirable: Will have a positive effect and little or no negative effect.	4
	Definitely infeasible: Cannot be implemented (unworkable).	0
	Probably infeasible: Some indication this cannot be implemented.	1
	May or may not be feasible: Contradictory evidence this can be implemented.	3

Table 33. *(Continued)*

Statement	Ratings	Total Number of Panelist Who Selected Each Ratings
	Probably feasible: Some indication this can be implemented.	3
	Definitely feasible: Can be implemented.	3

Table 34. Internal Control Activities UIPath Robot Processing 3rd Round Data: Non-consensus.

Statement	Ratings	Total Number of Panelist Who Selected Each Ratings
Statement 126 – Internal control activities towards capital regulation that can be effective in reducing losses includes use of UIPath robot processing is one area of automation that is a viable option.		
	Highly undesirable: Will have major negative effect.	0
	Undesirable: Will have a negative effect with little or no positive effect.	1
	Neither desirable nor undesirable: Will have equal positive and negative effects.	3
	Desirable: Will have a positive effect with minimum negative effects.	0

(Continued)

Table 34. *(Continued)*

Statement	Ratings	Total Number of Panelist Who Selected Each Ratings
	Highly desirable: Will have a positive effect and little or no negative effect.	2
	Definitely infeasible: Cannot be implemented (unworkable).	0
	Probably infeasible: Some indication this cannot be implemented.	0
	May or may not be feasible: Contradictory evidence this can be implemented	2
	Probably feasible: Some indication this can be implemented.	3
	Definitely feasible: Can be implemented.	3

compliance with the regulatory requirements (Allen et al., 2016). However, there are inaccuracies in running these models, and the results have produced errors and failed to alert management of risk and failure to breach guidelines. These inaccuracies in model risk predictions require further investigation (Crabb, 2018). Banks should consider linking scenarios and stress-testing processes that will capture bank's material risk exposures activities and strive to employ mitigating measures that are conceptually sound approaches (Lee, 2015). Additionally, there should be considerations to employ the use of third-party risk assessment and modelling tools that can help meet regulatory requirement and risk reduction measures (Lee, 2015).

On the other hand, banks that have deployed AIS find the system beneficial in gathering information use for financial statements, planning data, regulatory filing and meeting data request from regulators, and assist in the overall decision-making process (Baker et al., 2023). The digital and online data have changed how information is captured and shared in real time globally for banks, and AIS has used this avenue to capture data, process, stored and distribute data (Baker et al., 2023). The new technological developments Shi and Wang (2014) assert have placed network technology in high speed, and significant changes were made to commercial bank operation platforms. This new technological advancement will address the concern of Boora and Kavita (2018) that banks need strong technological infrastructure that will improve data quality, availability that can be upgraded and achieve regulatory requirements and filings. Many banks that are in the process of contemplating the change management process relating to their operations systems have to replace their systems as the old system cannot meet the speedy expansion of business scope and regulatory demands; the failures in their operation system and the need to have comprehensive coverage of all business risk leaves the bank with no other alternative but to look to automated control (Shi & Wang, 2014). However, systems are faced with the challenges of lack of technical support leading to systems breaches, bank accounting risk and significant harm to the business (Shi & Wang, 2014). The performance of the system, information quality efficacy and service quality is linked to the quality of help and training system users receive from the information systems organization and IT support personnel (Baker et al., 2023). Since banks operate globally, they have to bear in mind that IT support personnel and their teams should be equipped to service the multiple banks systems operation in various locations internationally. Polizzi and Scannella (2023) noted internal control systems need to be supported by information technology (IT) applications that makes it possible to access data from multiple systems and analyze data in meaningful ways that impact decision making in a timely manner. There are effective internal control activities relating to automation of processes and technology designed to mitigate risks within the control environment that the panel of experts reached consensus. These statements votes are displayed in Tables (35 and 36) (Velez, 2020).

Table 35. Internal Control Activities Key Performance/Risk Indicators 3rd Round Data: Consensus.

Statement	**Ratings**	**Total Number of Panelist Who Selected Each Ratings**
Statement 42 – Internal control activities towards capital regulation that can be effective in reducing losses includes monthly/quarterly reporting over controls performance to include key performance/risk indicators.		

(Continued)

Table 35. *(Continued)*

Statement	Ratings	Total Number of Panelist Who Selected Each Ratings
	Highly undesirable: Will have major negative effect.	0
	Undesirable: Will have a negative effect with little or no positive effect.	1
	Neither desirable nor undesirable: Will have equal positive and negative effects.	0
	Desirable: Will have a positive effect with minimum negative effects.	4
	Highly desirable: Will have a positive effect and little or no negative effect.	6
	Definitely infeasible: Cannot be implemented (unworkable).	1
	Probably infeasible: Some indication this cannot be implemented.	1
	May or may not be feasible: Contradictory evidence this can be implemented.	0
	Probably feasible: Some indication this can be implemented.	3
	Definitely feasible: Can be implemented.	4

The banks have to design internal controls that are monitoring activities that will alert them to changes in risk levels. Key risk indictors (KRIs) are key monitoring controls that bank deploy to monitor risk levels that should be

Table 36. Internal Control Activities Automation of Manual Processes 3rd Round Data: Consensus.

Statement	Ratings	Total Number of Panelist Who Selected Each Ratings
Statement 109 – Internal control activities towards capital regulation that can be effective in reducing losses includes automation of manual processes that are prone to human errors.		
	Highly undesirable: Will have major negative effect.	0
	Undesirable: Will have a negative effect with little or no positive effect.	2
	Neither desirable nor undesirable: Will have equal positive and negative effects.	1
	Desirable: Will have a positive effect with minimum negative effects.	3
	Highly desirable: Will have a positive effect and little or no negative effect.	6
	Definitely infeasible: Cannot be implemented (unworkable).	0
	Probably infeasible: Some indication this cannot be implemented.	0
	May or may not be feasible: Contradictory evidence this can be implemented.	4
	Probably feasible: Some indication this can be implemented.	3
	Definitely feasible: Can be implemented.	3

supported by reliable IT systems, that can retrieve, slice and dice the data. IT applications analyze data use to generate system indicators and KRIs; the identification and computation of these indicators associate the events of risk captured in the data processed daily to annually (Polizzi & Scannella, 2023). These indicators alert management on the level of riskiness of the processes and potential threat to the business (Polizzi & Scannella, 2023). Key risk indicators are metrics used that provide evidence of an early warning of increase/decrease of risk levels; this identifies what processes have high levels of risk and potential threat to business continuity (Polizzi & Scannella, 2023). The results of these indicators equipped process owners with information on the performance of key and non-key controls; these indicators should be equipped with definition of thresholds and how to interpret their results (Polizzi & Scannella, 2023). Additionally, the use of trend analyses can be utilized to perform routine trend analyses that monitor indicator trends and obtain early warning signals that will equip management to implement timely corrective actions (Polizzi & Scannella, 2023). RegTech was recommended as another useful technology system for banks to use to meet various requirements; prudential risk management, compliance, capital optimization, trading, portfolio management and cybersecurity (Lai, 2018).

RegTech enables banks to find a solution to their challenges faced in complying with new and amended regulations, meeting time deadlines posed by the Basel Committee's (Lai, 2018). Banks can use RegTech to automate this process and reduce manual intervention, comply with Basel Committee's guidelines on bank risk data aggregation (Lai, 2018). This will support the growth of transparency and efficiency between financial institutions and regulators who will be able to monitor and analyze real-time financial information from multinational banks throughout the global financial sector. This would strengthen the initiative of regulators to create a safer and more efficient financial system. Meager (2017) support the use of technology as a tool that will enable banks to comply with regulation compliance requirements. The use of technology will provide banks with cost savings in reducing the time it takes to product the reporting and filing of the compliance documentation required by the regulators (Meager, 2017). RegTech developments as best harness in automation of mass administrative tasks imposed by the regulatory environment (Meager, 2017). There are some gaps in RegTech that should not be ignored pointed out by Kavassalis et al. (2018) that RegTech potential inadequate handling of risk data and the human component involved in the utilization of RegTech. Banks should be mindful of RegTech compliance cost and the production of supervisory reporting (Kavassalis et al., 2018).

Furthermore, HSBC Group Head of Innovation mentioned RegTech as a technological solution to regulatory requirements and filings that banks need to be in compliance; RegTech enables automation of processes, risk identification efficiencies and meet regulatory requirements (Barberis & Buckley, 2017). Global financial institutions and their regulators can access, monitor and analyze real-time financial information which will effectuate an efficient financial system.

Chapter 10

Risk Identification and Communication

Banks are exposed to risk domestically and globally stemming from the business environment in which they execute their transactions, the nature of these goods and services, individuals executing the processes, laws and regulations that govern the execution of these activities, and the technology/system used to carry out these business events. The company analyzes these varied factors of risk embedded in its transactions which is a significant part of the risk identification process used to identify the What Can Go Wrong in the execution of its business activities. Risk assessment process is used to identify current risk and emerging risk the bank faces when conducting business. Hamed (2023) noted risk assessment is a critical process within the internal control system (ICS) which performs a detailed analysis of potential risks and the execution of actionable steps/items to managing these risks. The assessment of the potential impact of risks and creation of controls to mitigate them, reduces the likelihood of adverse events (Hamed, 2023). The ICS function is critical to the banking industry as it facilitate operational effectiveness, trustworthy financial information, adherence to legal requirements and regulations, and asset protection (Hamed, 2023). The banking sector is service oriented and relies on human decision making, interpret and application of regulations, which reinforces the importance of ICS in compliance (Hamed, 2023). A weak ICS influence employee in the banking sectors to commit acts such as, fraud practices, unethical behaviours; on the other hand, a strong ICS has the ability to identify the types of practices that form a risk event to the bank through risk identification measures (Hamed, 2023).

Bank management employs risk assessment strategies to identify current risk and emerging risk as part of their identification process. Risk identification covers internal factors (institutional account structure, corresponding contracts, nature of institutional activities, institution's human resources quality, organizational changes, employee turnover) and external factors (industry changes, technological advances) which is imperative to monitoring risk and building the control environment (Izhar & Asutay, 2010). Similarly, Hamed (2023) posits banks faces numerous types of risk from internal sources (unethical practices reflected in financial data preparation, management regulations), and external sources (related to industry) that should be assessed and an evaluation of impact

Effective Internal Control Practices in Banks, 127–135

Published under exclusive licence by Emerald Publishing Limited
doi:10.1108/978-1-83662-972-620251013

performed. The risk assessment when carried out examines and analyzes activities that identify and manage uncertain events align to external and internal factors (Abiola & Oyewole, 2013). The identification and analysis of risks should be weighed against the bank's achievement of its objectives and the respective mitigating measures; Khalil and Hasan (2020) assert risk identification and its management should be inclusive of assessment of risk profiles, relationships of risk events, measurement of the risk exposure, frequency of these events, and materiality of these risk events. These many complex and varied forms of risk factors need to be brought in concert when looking at risk identification. A part of the risk identification is to document the risk and identify internal controls to mitigate the occurrence of the identified risk. An effective risk assessment relies on the establishment of objectives that are coherent and interconnected at all levels within the organization; furthermore, the constant changes (economic, industry, regulatory, operational conditions) within the industry need to be monitored the use of mechanisms that can identify, and address risks associated with these changes (Hamed, 2023).

Abiola and Oyewole (2013) maintain the risk management initiative encompasses internal control functions that includes considerations of internal and external threats when creating mitigation activities and measures. Banks utilize a risk management framework to carry out its risk identification process and communicate the result to the respective stakeholders. A risk management framework incorporates risks identification, measurement, assessment of risk exposure, control mitigation activities, monitoring and reporting results to stakeholders (PRIMER: Operational risk – prudential regulation perspective, 2018). The risk management system should address the process use to assess employees and process owners, measure/monitor enhancements and process improvements, risk prevention measures within the bank, and management including risk awareness as an inseparable with daily activity within their daily task and operations (Shi & Wang, 2014). There are tools the banks used in the risk assessment and monitoring process such as risk and control self-assessment (RCSA), business process mapping, internal loss data collection and analysis, external loss data analysis, key risk indicator (KRI), and scenario analysis (PRIMER: Operational risk – prudential regulation perspective, 2018). Rahim et al. (2018) noted risk management should include the examination, review and documentation of policies, system tools, processes, procedures, management oversight and supervision to mitigate known and unknown risks. Risk identification and mitigation measures should take into account in the examination process past loss events, successful and unsuccessful risk goals and the challenges improvements to operational efficiency, bank management processing risks, quality of services to customers and opportunities for improvement, and information and human resources management (Rahim et al., 2018). People risk as noted by Hamed (2023) is an important contributor to internal risks that should not be overlooked; this stems from the lack of qualified accounting staff with technical expertise in Securities and Exchange Commission (SEC) regulations, SOX, and Generally Accepted Accounting Principles (GAAP). This lack of technical knowledge has direct impact on the results of internal control being ineffective (Hamed, 2023).

An all-inclusive approach should be deployed when identifying potential risk and designing an effective risk management framework that have mitigation measures and activities to address the many idiosyncrasies of the risk management system. Ko et al. (2019) contends there need to be transparency in the execution of control activities, visibility in how the controls were carried out without impediment to address the risk identified. The risk management framework is complex structure that covers the internal control functions of the bank. These internal control functions are evidenced in internal control activities supported in the company's policies and procedures (Abiola & Oyewole, 2013). Similarly, Baker et al. (2023) placed emphasis on internal control functions manifested in the bank's policy with the objective of protecting the company's assets from misuse, correctness of information, guarantee applicable laws and regulations are followed. Internal control activities work to ensure there is consistency, reliability, credibility, and transparency in the company's activities processed. Maksimovic et al. (2023) asserts policies ensure employees follow the guidelines of management and control mechanisms of the organizational; policies document a clear definition of roles and responsibilities, segregation of duties, check and balances, documentation that justifies actions, compliance with regulatory rules and monitoring of information systems security. Having sound controls as articulated in the policies and procedures ensures reperformance of the company's activities required internally by senior management or externally by regulators (SEC, Feds); this task can be accomplished without placing stress on the daily activities of the bank and its's employees.

The examination of internal control objectives entails maintaining a bank environment that deter events from occurring by accident or on purpose (Baker et al., 2023). Bank's transactions should be processed intentionally using senior management approved internal control processes documented in the policies adopted, and making judgements (Baker et al., 2023). Control activities are one of the components of internal control function and systems deployed in carrying out management actionable items; control activities, enforce rules, procedures, and sanctions for potential risks when they develop (Baker et al., 2023). The ICS ensure vital economic events are collected by the accounting information system (AIS) which compiles the company's data in its pure form without alteration and errors are collection important sectors of the internal control function (Baker et al., 2023). Risk identification examines all these different players (AIS, ICS, Control Activities, Individual processors) that can compromise the company and exposed the company to significant risks resulting in losses, reputational damage and findings.

Internal control activities are needed to design and improve company's culture, technology, management/process owners' actions, operation scale, personnel quality, internal control cost, and the monitoring and communication of control test results (Shi & Wang, 2014). The design of the controls (preventative, detective, monitoring, automated, manual, timing, frequency) and documentation of these controls is necessary for the effective operation of these controls. Internal control activities design and operating effectiveness are relevant to maintain a sustainable system and process; de Jongh et al. (2013) mentioned Institutions have implemented fraud detection systems to detect and prevent fraudulent acts carried out by external third parties. Timeliness is an important ingredient in identifying breakdown of controls performance and the risk impact, as this allows management to mitigate and prevent damages to the company from occurring and expanding. For example, control activities failure to prevent unauthorized transaction at Irish Allied Irisk Bank (AIB) resulted in losses of $700 mn in the foreign exchange market in 2001; Republic New York Corporation customer fraud resulted in a loss of $611 million (Anouar et al., 2017). The fraudulent wording use in financial protection products and insurance legal documents resulting in losses of UK banks £264 million in 2011 (de Jongh et al., 2013). These failed controls and risk should be identified and communicated to respective stakeholders in a timely manner. Information and communication risk identification, control performance, capture/recording of activities, exchange of financial data, operational and compliance-related data should be completed in a timely manner; it is important to monitor the quality of the internal control activities performance and identify gaps in the execution in a timely manner (Abiola & Oyewole, 2013). There are effective internal control activities relating to risk identification and information and communication that the panel of experts reached consensus. These statements votes are displayed below Tables (37–39) (Velez, 2020).

Table 37. Internal Control Activities Establish Communication Expectations 3rd Round Data: Consensus.

Statement	Ratings	Total Number of Panelist Who Selected Each Ratings
Statement 41 – Internal control activities towards capital regulation that can be effective in reducing losses includes established expectations for communication and reporting.		
	Highly undesirable: Will have major negative effect.	0
	Undesirable: Will have a negative effect with little or no positive effect.	0

Table 37. *(Continued)*

Statement	Ratings	Total Number of Panelist Who Selected Each Ratings
	Neither desirable nor undesirable: Will have equal positive and negative effects.	2
	Desirable: Will have a positive effect with minimum negative effects.	2
	Highly desirable: Will have a positive effect and little or no negative effect.	6
	Definitely infeasible: Cannot be implemented (unworkable).	0
	Probably infeasible: Some indication this cannot be implemented.	1
	May or may not be feasible: Contradictory evidence this can be implemented.	1
	Probably feasible: Some indication this can be implemented.	5
	Definitely feasible: Can be implemented.	4

In order for ICS to effectively mitigate the identified risks, there need to be continuous cooperation between all supervisory authority, internal and external auditors supported with periodic meetings (Repousis et al., 2019). Business face challenges in their implementation of internal controls. Hamed (2023) asserts small businesses in implementing internal controls face challenges stemming from the lack of resources, skills, and awareness. However, it should be noted a proficient risk management strategy can assist banks in attaining viable long-term success.

Table 38. Internal Control Activities Communication in Entire Organization 3rd Round Data: Consensus.

Statement	Ratings	Total Number of Panelist Who Selected Each Ratings
Statement 94 – Risk management practices towards capital regulation that can be effective in reducing losses includes communication within the entire organization.		
	Highly undesirable: Will have major negative effect.	0
	Undesirable: Will have a negative effect with little or no positive effect.	0
	Neither desirable nor undesirable: Will have equal positive and negative effects.	4
	Desirable: Will have a positive effect with minimum negative effects.	1
	Highly desirable: Will have a positive effect and little or no negative effect.	2
	Definitely infeasible: Cannot be implemented (unworkable).	0
	Probably infeasible: Some indication this cannot be implemented.	0
	May or may not be feasible: Contradictory evidence this can be implemented.	4
	Probably feasible: Some indication this can be implemented.	2

Table 38. *(Continued)*

Statement	Ratings	Total Number of Panelist Who Selected Each Ratings
	Definitely feasible: Can be implemented.	2
	Highly undesirable: Will have major negative effect.	0

Table 39. Internal Control Activities Independent Risk Identification 3rd Round Data: Consensus.

Statement	Ratings	Total Number of Panelist Who Selected Each Ratings
Statement 121 – Risk management practices towards capital regulation that can be effective in reducing losses includes an independent risk identification and management.		
	Highly undesirable: Will have major negative effect.	0
	Undesirable: Will have a negative effect with little or no positive effect.	1
	Neither desirable nor undesirable: Will have equal positive and negative effects.	1
	Desirable: Will have a positive effect with minimum negative effects.	4

(Continued)

Table 39. *(Continued)*

Statement	Ratings	Total Number of Panelist Who Selected Each Ratings
	Highly desirable: Will have a positive effect and little or no negative effect.	6
	Definitely infeasible: Cannot be implemented (unworkable).	0
	Probably infeasible: Some indication this cannot be implemented.	0
	May or may not be feasible: Contradictory evidence this can be implemented.	1
	Probably feasible: Some indication this can be implemented.	4
	Definitely feasible: Can be implemented.	4

There needs to be collaboration among stakeholders on the management of risk through effective information and communication.

Information and Communication include identifies, process and communicate information to all the stakeholders upward and downward levels throughout the bank; this process continuously inform them about changes at all levels (Chowdhury, 2021). An effective information and communication system validates the authenticity of the information, reliability, and disseminated in a timely manner to the appropriate decision makers internally and externally (Chowdhury, 2021). Information and communication are one of the pillars effective internal control rests on (Al-Hawatmeh, 2021). The sustainability of effective internal control and meeting structural goals depends on the quality of information (pertinent, trustworthy, complete, timely) and communication to the respective stakeholders internally and externally Hamed (2023). Information and communication relating the internal control process (identification, capture, exchange of financial, operational, compliance-related data) should be done in a timely manner; this is just as important as monitoring the quality of the internal control activities to identify breakdown in the control system timely (Abiola & Oyewole, 2013). This will allow management to pivot on immediate matters deemed high risk and take responsive measures in a timely manner. The timeliness can reduce potential impact and damages from risk identified, losses, or the magnitude of fines where applicable. There are efficiencies to banks when effective communication is practiced; this is evident in the sharing of financial information to groups within the bank on the organization's performance which allows them to take reactive measures if needed, and it reduced the potential for opportunistic behaviour by managers (Hamed, 2023). The banks financial performance can be influenced by information and communication when there is effectiveness ICS and the alignment of promoting the alignment of shareholders and managers interest in championing long-term organizational success (Hamed, 2023). The application of effective communication and information enhances several factors (transparency, accountability, reputation) with in the bank that is sustainable (Hamed, 2023). Banks should invest more in sustainability initiatives that puts information and communication at the forefront of its objectives in meeting performance goals and maintenance of competitive edge (Hamed, 2023).

Chapter 11

Timely Reporting and Escalation

The receipt of timely information shared through communication channels such as reporting, assessments, audit results is crucial for the various stakeholders to react and take responsive measures to prevent identified issues from progressing materially. Shi and Wang (2014) posit timely detection and treatment is essential in managing accounting risk and the practice of effective control of regulation. The use of severe punishment afterwards as remedies simply does not work in the prevention of accounting risk (Shi &Wang, 2014). The lack of effectiveness in the assessment of common problems of accounting risk contributes to issues not being predicted timely, and prevention measures cannot be undertaken by the responsible departments (Shi &Wang, 2014). Bank management performs assessment of threats to financial reporting integrity, reliability and accuracy within the control environment; the underlining risk is identified and analysed to determine the impact on timely financial reporting (Salameh, 2019). This assessment is used as supporting documentation for the risk response and the action plans to mitigate risk (Salameh, 2019). The bank's Board of Directors plays an important role in ensuring timely reporting information is shared both internally and externally by reviewing this information and setting a tolerance level/temperature for the sharing of good quality reporting information. The methodology used by the bank to assess risk is reviewed and approved by the Board of Directors which ensures the document is free of bias and is a credible risk assessment document (Duncan, 2021). This enterprise-wide risk assessment (EWRA) methodology document covers the institution's risk appetite, alignment to the bank's tolerance levels, purpose and direction, measurement approach, identification and management of risks that is over-the-tolerance levels (Duncan, 2021). The Board of Directors sets the frequencies for meeting to discuss the results of risk tolerances levels monitored through indicators and the level of detail reporting required for those meetings to inform management of areas that need action plans. The Board of Directors role is articulated in the methodology document four sections: section one documents board of directors role related to risk stipulated in the policy statement/roles and responsibilities of individuals/stakeholders in the execution of EWRA and risk culture; second section focuses on Risk Model and eight areas in risk assessment/scoring; third section discusses (administrative

Effective Internal Control Practices in Banks, 137–146

doi:10.1108/978-1-83662-972-620251014

reporting line, sanctioning, frequency of EWRA, approval) maintenance; fourth section highlights information relating to assessors (Duncan, 2021).

The company's Board of Directors work with senior management and other employees in obtaining reasonable assurance on reliable financial reporting information, that will assist the bank in the achievement of effectiveness and efficiency of operations (Hamed, 2023). Ghosh (2021) asserts Board of Directors and the regulators receiving timely periodic reports based on the monitoring reviews within the bank are required for an effective internal control environment. Furthermore, Ghosh (2021) posits it is the responsibility of the Board of Directors to oversee the institution crucial functions, risk management and ensure the bank's control environment is effective. As such, potential issues should be detected, shared and escalated in a timely manner to respective parties to take actions to ensure reliable financial reporting on time (Hamed, 2023). Hideaki and Naoki (2021) noted one of the benefits of better-quality financial reporting is it reduces information asymmetry. Banks who suffer from the lack of timey reporting suffer from information disproportionateness which has caused them to incur significant losses, failure to mitigate risk timely, reputational damage and regulatory findings. Information asymmetry among bank stakeholders contributed to significant loses (Abou-El-Sood, 2017). There is a lack of timely and current corporate reporting that meets the need of the investment community; the reports shared were inadequate for decision-making, confusing, cluttered, fragmented, disconnected, complex and suffering from inadequate information (Stubbs & Higgins, 2018). The accounting information system (AIS) can help to remediate the data quality issues and timeliness in reporting when conducted with effective internal controls. Baker et al. (2023) posit AIS should provide timely accurate, reliable, trustworthy information to its users; to ensure sustainability of timely accurate information, bank should implement acceptable internal control with prioritization given to system- and employee-related issues. As a computer-based system, the AIS maintains the quality of accounting data, boosts control, improves collaboration, data visibility, accessibility to stakeholders (Baker et al., 2023).

Bank management needs timely and detailed internal control to effectively direct the organization towards achieving its established goals and business development (Maksimovic et al., 2023). Banks should run the computation of the indicators for the associated risk events in a timely manner; this is essential to determine the level of risk in the processes and take appropriate actions to curtail it's expansion (Polizzi & Scannella, 2023). Risk indicators provide early warning signs when the level of risk within a process is too high, and the process owners can use the computations for the evaluation of internal controls (Polizzi & Scannella, 2023). Bank senior management establish definitions and thresholds used to interpret the data, early warning signals and recommend timely corrective actions; these definitions help them understand the trend analyses performed and indicator trend results (Polizzi & Scannella, 2023). Management can react to stop the increase in the company's exposure to a particular risk if they receive credible information of these types of events and their root causes in early onset. There are past instances where senior management were not notified of a risk event timely and the loss exposure grew to material amounts causing the company to experience significant losses. The lack of timely information and transparency in reporting on a growing risk event at JP Morgan in the trading department causes the company to suffer more than $2 billion in trading losses in 2012 (Shorter et al., 2012). These losses related to financial derivatives in 2012 that were used to unwind a previous hedge investment too late after loss event already grew enormously in size (Shorter et al., 2012). One of the senior management, the CIO of JP Morgan, did not receive data on the risk event timely and reacted to the late information on the event by placing a new counter-hedge position instead of getting rid of the original index tied to credit default swaps (Shorter et al., 2012). The second hedge on a hedge caused the risk to grow to a larger risk exposure resulting to significant losses (Shorter et al., 2012). The late actions by senior management of JP Morgan on the credit default swap risk event was tied to lack of timely reporting and transparency to the risk event root causes. The passing of Sarbanes–Oxley (SOX) Act 2002 was to assist in the identification of fraud and errors in a timely manner as part of the annual SOX audit and management attestations on the state of their internal controls. In some cases, SOX aided in the early detection and prosecution of fraud.

Two months after the passing and enactment of SOX Act 2002, there was an investigation of HealthSouth CEO relating to the companies' reporting of earnings which was fraudulently overstated by $1.4 billion which began in 1999 (Stigliano, 2011). Several HealthSouth executives were involved with the commitment of fraud of up to $2.5 billion in earnings which was credited to SOX for the actions to be caught and identified timely when compared to other companies' fraudulent acts that went undetected for several years (Stigliano, 2011). Several US officials asserted that the deployment of SOX has contributed to corporate-fraud prosecutions and fraud identification in an effective and efficient time (Stigliano, 2011). Timely reporting of risk exposure and fraud has been regarded as an area that needs continuous improvement in the banking and financial services industry. There is delay in reporting the exposure to senior management, instead a cover up of the losses and risk is the avenue pursued. The panel of expert votes, non-consensus and consensus, are displayed in Tables (40–44).

Table 40. Internal Control Activities Reporting Activities Timely 3rd Round Data: Non-consensus.

Statement	**Ratings**	**Total Number of Panelist Who Selected Each Ratings**
Statement 5 – Internal control activities towards capital regulation that can be effective in reducing losses includes reporting activities timely.		
	Highly undesirable: Will have major negative effect.	1

(Continued)

Table 40. *(Continued)*

Statement	Ratings	Total Number of Panelist Who Selected Each Ratings
	Undesirable: Will have a negative effect with little or no positive effect.	0
	Neither desirable nor undesirable: Will have equal positive and negative effects.	2
	Desirable: Will have a positive effect with minimum negative effects.	1
	Highly desirable: Will have a positive effect and little or no negative effect.	5
	Definitely infeasible: Cannot be implemented (unworkable).	0
	Probably infeasible: Some indication this cannot be implemented.	1
	May or may not be feasible: Contradictory evidence this can be implemented.	3
	Probably feasible: Some indication this can be implemented.	3
	Definitely feasible: Can be implemented.	5

The company's Board of Directors, senior management and other employees will need to work together in the sustaining and reporting on an effective internal control system (Hamed, 2023). The act of fraud and material risks grows in a weak control environment with poor oversight committees and insufficient supervisory initiatives traders (Parnes, 2014). Trade frauds and misstated

Table 41. Internal Control Activities Reporting of Exposure Timely 3rd Round Data: Non-consensus.

Statement	Ratings	Total Number of Panelist Who Selected Each Ratings
Statement 6 – Internal control activities towards capital regulation that can be effective in reducing losses includes timely reporting of exposure.		
	Highly undesirable: Will have major negative effect.	1
	Undesirable: Will have a negative effect with little or no positive effect.	1
	Neither desirable nor undesirable: Will have equal positive and negative effects.	1
	Desirable: Will have a positive effect with minimum negative effects.	1
	Highly desirable: Will have a positive effect and little or no negative effect.	5
	Definitely infeasible: Cannot be implemented (unworkable).	0
	Probably infeasible: Some indication this cannot be implemented.	0
	May or may not be feasible: Contradictory evidence this can be implemented.	1
	Probably feasible: Some indication this can be implemented.	7
	Definitely feasible: Can be implemented.	4

Table 42. Internal Control Activities Reporting Capital Effects Timely 3rd Round Data: Non-consensus.

Statement	Ratings	Total Number of Panelist Who Selected Each Ratings
Statement 7 – Internal control activities towards capital regulation that can be effective in reducing losses includes iimely reporting of potential capital effects will go a long way towards reducing losses in bank holding companies.		
	Highly undesirable: Will have major negative effect.	0
	Undesirable: Will have a negative effect with little or no positive effect.	1
	Neither desirable nor undesirable: Will have equal positive and negative effects.	1
	Desirable: Will have a positive effect with minimum negative effects.	4
	Highly desirable: Will have a positive effect and little or no negative effect.	3
	Definitely infeasible: Cannot be implemented (unworkable).	0
	Probably infeasible: Some indication this cannot be implemented.	0
	May or may not be feasible: Contradictory evidence this can be implemented.	1

Table 42. *(Continued)*

Statement	Ratings	Total Number of Panelist Who Selected Each Ratings
	Probably feasible: Some indication this can be implemented.	6
	Definitely feasible: Can be implemented.	3

Table 43. Internal Control Activities Strong Governance Committees 3rd Round Data: Consensus.

Statement	Ratings	Total Number of Panelist Who Selected Each Ratings
Statement 39 – Internal control activities towards capital regulation that can be effective in reducing losses includes strong governance committees.		
	Highly undesirable: Will have major negative effect.	1
	Undesirable: Will have a negative effect with little or no positive effect.	0
	Neither desirable nor undesirable: Will have equal positive and negative effects.	1
	Desirable: Will have a positive effect with minimum negative effects.	1
	Highly desirable: Will have a positive effect and little or no negative effect.	6

(Continued)

Table 43. *(Continued)*

Statement	Ratings	Total Number of Panelist Who Selected Each Ratings
	Definitely infeasible: Cannot be implemented (unworkable).	1
	Probably infeasible: Some indication this cannot be implemented.	1
	May or may not be feasible: Contradictory evidence this can be implemented.	2
	Probably feasible: Some indication this can be implemented.	4
	Definitely feasible: Can be implemented.	3

Table 44. Internal Control Activities Reporting and Escalation 3rd Round Data: Non-consensus.

Statement	Ratings	Total Number of Panelist Who Selected Each Ratings
Statement 40 – Internal control activities towards capital regulation that can be effective in reducing losses includes reporting and escalation.		
	Highly undesirable: Will have major negative effect.	0
	Undesirable: Will have a negative effect with little or no positive effect.	0

Table 44. *(Continued)*

Statement	Ratings	Total Number of Panelist Who Selected Each Ratings
	Neither desirable nor undesirable: Will have equal positive and negative effects.	1
	Desirable: Will have a positive effect with minimum negative effects.	2
	Highly desirable: Will have a positive effect and little or no negative effect.	7
	Definitely infeasible: Cannot be implemented (unworkable).	0
	Probably infeasible: Some indication this cannot be implemented.	1
	May or may not be feasible: Contradictory evidence this can be implemented.	2
	Probably feasible: Some indication this can be implemented.	4
	Definitely feasible: Can be implemented.	3

financials are activities that lack transparency of market transactions, unauthorized positions offset by fake positions and other concealment techniques and intentional reporting information to mislead the public on the financial health of the company (Hagen et al., 2020). The rate manipulation/LIBOR scandal at Barclays Bank, Citigroup, Deutsche Bank, JPMorgan, Lloyds Bank, Royal Bank of Scotland, UBS activities went undetected for more than two years, causing significant damage of more than USD 1.5 bn and the end of jail sentence of 5 years or more (Hagen et al., 2020). These types of activities have increased the need for financial regulators to globally crackdown on fraud that is harmful to the capital markets (Montagano, 2012). Company's internal control activities are designed to detect inappropriate capturing and recording of individual transactions collected into account balances and financial results (Stigliano, 2011). While the identification and reporting of an issue and/or risk is good, it must be followed up with actionable mitigation plans, escalation and strong governance committees. Public companies have oversight committees that examine and review the work of management who are decision-makers/process owners of the finance functions, corporate strategies and profits (Stigliano, 2011). These oversight committees receive monthly and quarterly reporting packages of the finance functions and financial reports of the business. The committee identifies issues and replaces management who fail to implement effective solution; in some instances, corporate frauds are committed by managers, CEO and CFO who create fraudulent financial statements (Stigliano, 2011).

Chapter 12

Internal Control Effective Practices

Internal control practices that are effective made significant positive impacts on the bank's control environment reflected in its risk management programmes, financial reporting, oversight committees, meeting regulatory requirements and the overall profitability of the organization. Aksoy and Mohammed (2020) assert internal control functions have become a safety device to ensure stakeholders' objectives, business goals, corporate governance, quality assurance, corporate risk management (CRM), transparency, accuracy, accountability, sustainability and competitive nature are met. Internal controls guarantee management fulfilment of their duties to stakeholders in the correct manner and transparency in financial statements (Aksoy & Mohammed, 2020). An effective internal control system ensures consistency in the processes in which the bank carries out its business. The bank is not operating in project mode all the time and putting out fire drills; on the contrary, the bank's activities are processed based on procedures and policy that articulates the acceptable practices for conducting business. A feasible internal control framework is the essential backbone of a company and serves as a key relevant aspect of organization's policies globally (Aksoy & Mohammed, 2020). It was noted by Abou-El-Sood (2017) that banks with good governance have adequate information, quality supporting documentation, healthy financial performance and results, manage their risk and undertake less risky. Regulators in the United States and globally have taken note of the benefits of internal control and governance on the bank control environment as a result of the laws they have passed. Hamed (2023) noted the passing of Sarbanes–Oxley (SOX) Act 2002 has a direct impact on the enhancement of internal controls for publicly listed firms and the quality of their reporting and financial statements.

Banks are required to have strong governance and control mechanisms reflected in board and senior management oversight, policies and procedures, controls and compliance (Goldberg, 2017). It was noted by the New York State Control Task Force Report that internal control principles are embedded in organizational structured techniques and principles (Aksoy & Mohammed, 2020). Banks with effective internal control fosters competitive advantage, manage risk effectively, create action plans that facilitate the companies' aims, and achieve

Effective Internal Control Practices in Banks, 147–153

doi:10.1108/978-1-83662-972-620251015

stakeholders' goals (Aksoy & Mohammed, 2020). A systematic rigorous and quick-responding internal control system can prevent supervision loopholes, lessen conditions favourable to non-compliance, restrict opportunistic behaviour, lessen the chances of committing misconduct and reduce litigation risks (Chen et al., 2023). Similarly, companies that have good internal controls experience consistent reliable reporting, adherence to relevant laws and regulations, bolster integrity of all forms of information, and long-term growth of the firm with high level of confidence (Hamed, 2023). There are effective internal control activities that the panel of experts reached consensus as effective, namely relating to strong governance committees, reporting and escalation, expectations for communication and reporting, time to recognize problems and follow procedures and won't cut corners when they are not always under extreme pressure, automation of manual processes that are prone to human errors, monthly/quarterly reporting over controls performance to include key performance/risk indicators, periodic risk and controls assessment, training a priority and having a Risk Taxonomy to mitigate risks within the control environment that the panel of experts reached consensus. The consensus level set at 6 out of 10 votes; these statements votes are displayed in Table 45 (Velez, 2020).

Table 45. Internal Control Statements That Satisfied Consensus Threshold in Round 3.

Statement	**Rating (Desirability)**	**Rating (Feasibility)**
Internal control activities towards capital regulation that can be effective in reducing losses includes strong governance committees.	6	4
Internal control activities towards capital regulation that can be effective in reducing losses includes reporting and escalation.	7	4
Internal control activities towards capital regulation that can be effective in reducing losses includes established expectations for communication and reporting.	6	5
Internal control activities towards capital regulation that can be effective in reducing losses includes ensuring employees have time to recognise problems and follow procedures and won't cut corners when they are not always under extreme pressure.	6	2

Table 45. *(Continued)*

Statement	Rating (Desirability)	Rating (Feasibility)
Internal control activities towards capital regulation that can be effective in reducing losses includes automation of manual processes that are prone to human errors.	6	4
Internal control activities towards capital regulation that can be effective in reducing losses include monthly/quarterly reporting over controls performance to include key performance/risk indicators.	6	4
Internal control activities towards capital regulation that can be effective in reducing losses includes periodic risk and controls assessment.	6	5
Internal control activities towards capital regulation that can be effective in reducing losses includes making training a priority.	6	5
Internal control activities towards capital regulation that can be effective in reducing losses includes having a Risk Taxonomy.	7	4

These control activities when implemented and monitored timely can bring efficiencies and good results in the banking industry. Banks should implement strong governance committees to mitigate the risk Stigliano (2011) noted in poor corporate governance as one of the main causes of poor performance, manipulated financial reports and displeased stakeholder. The structure and design of corporate governance sets the tone at the top where leaders of the organization uphold ethics and integrity, and followers/employees will emulate these activities (Stigliano, 2011). A firm that has poor corporate governance focuses primarily on checks and balances at the top of the organization hierarchy mainly at top levels (board of directors, top management) a type of imbalance of power in favour of top management evidenced in firms, such as Enron, Tyco and WorldCom which led to these companies' downfalls. It is imperative to have Boards and Committees independent of each other. An ineffective board and its committees that are careless supervisors of management incentivize fraud, scandals, financial statements manipulation, use of off-balance sheet financing that had board participation in concealing the distorted statements because they lacked independence from senior management (Al-Matari et al., 2017). Similarly, World Com had overstatement of earnings leading to bankruptcy because there were failures in the audit committee (AC) supervising management (Al-Matari et al., 2017). A strong governance committee will have checks and balances in place, functions independently and will ensure leaders do not abuse their power.

Reporting and escalation have been noted by the panel of experts as effective practice to reduce/mitigate internal control risk. There should be timeliness in reporting issues noted that could expose the bank to greater risk; significant risk that has the potential to be systemic need clear instructions on the escalation process. Shi and Wang (2014) assert bank should take problem rectification seriously and have strict procedures on how to address the matter and improve their information exchange process and procedures. As such, the company should put focus/awareness on the rectification and educate stakeholders and employees on the subject (Shi & Wang, 2014). Additionally, banks should establish and improve mechanism, reinforce the follow-up tracking check to safeguard the rectification in place is functioning after the problem was identified (Shi & Wang, 2014). Information and communication were voted as effective internal control activities. Information should be presented with clarity and credibility and communicated throughout a workplace environment that does not operate in silos. An environment that operates in silos impedes communication effectiveness and brings harm to the bank. Helena and Madsen (2021) mentioned workplace silos are developed when employees work in a vacuum with little interaction/communication with other teams. This wall of isolation created by silos enforces lack of cooperation/communication between different risk and controls teams, gaps in accountability and communication with business units, causing redundancies and chaos to spread throughout the organization (Helena & Madsen, 2021). As such, Shi and Wang (2014) assert banks must create unhindered information communication and feedback channels, good internal controls atmosphere, and timely carry out the superior instructions and feedback at a lower level.

Bank employees are known to cut corners and skip important control steps to move transaction processing along to meet time deadlines. A complex process that is manual and relies on excel spreadsheet to process it's data falls vulnerable to employee cutting corners, forgoing critical procedures and steps to get the transaction completed compromising accuracy and completeness. The panel of experts reach consensus on the following internal control activities, ensuring employees have time to recognize problems, follow procedures and won't cut corners when they are not always under extreme pressure, automation of manual processes that are prone to human errors, quarterly reporting over controls performance to include key performance/risk indicators. Shi and Wang (2014) suggest banks implement a responsibility system that manages these identified risks and the related controls aligned to a clear responsibility chain. Potential problems should be identified timely with detailed documentation by item and follow-up procedures and feedback; this identification process should be business specific, possible risk and positive and effective control measures taken in advance (Shi & Wang, 2014). Abou-El-Sood (2017) and Boora and Kavita (2018) assert the management of risk is good governance practice during times of economic turmoil and increase the resiliency of banks. Risk management is an essential requirement which is in alignment with the panel of experts suggestions which includes the following; periodic risk and controls assessment, risk taxonomy, and training as effective internal control practices banks should implement. Banks need to have key controls that monitor banks capital which is essential to maintaining sufficient capital; this allows banks to have adequate provision for loan losses (Petersen et al., 2009). Banks with sufficient capital can mitigate the effects of financial shocks during financial crisis and recessions (Petersen et al., 2009). Bank manager should exercise prudency when utilizing idiosyncratic banking risk models as part of their capital monitoring initiatives; this should be done in concert with market discipline that is both credible and effective (Petersen et al., 2009). The management of risk is a complex process, and management should ensure that all areas are covered, namely risk relating to capital, assets and liabilities, strategic planning, implementation processes that control the volumes, diversity, maturity, interest rate sensitivity, quality, liquidity of assets, systemic risk, liabilities of the banking and financial system (Nitescu & Duna, 2016).

Abou-El-Sood (2017) and Boora and Kavita (2018) draw attention to imperative matters that should be examined when reviewing risk management in bank such as risk management efforts that monitor economic climate and trading. As noted by Walaa and Tucker (2016), risk management efforts have to be sensitive to the country's economic policies that require stronger mandatory requirements to ensure legitimate banking activities, legal systems that need improvements for independent risk management to overcome bank risk exposure from laws. Countries such as Czech Republic banking sector benefited from capital regulatory laws evident in capital ratio in these banks revealed they were well capitalized and remained profitable during the reporting period, which mitigated cyclical and structural risks (Pfeifer et al., 2017). Czech bank relationship used monitoring tools that examine risk weights, capital, leverage ratio increase of the risk weights decreased the capital ratio, increased the leverage ratio and capital reacts to the risk shock (Pfeifer et al., 2017). Similarly, regulatory bank laws in Brazil have been effective; it was noted these banks are closer to the regulatory minimum, relatively more risk-averse, make larger positive adjustments to their capital levels and smaller adjustments to their portfolio risk levels (Pereira & Saito, 2015). Additionally, low-capitalized banks manage their solvency ratios actively and keep capital and risk adjustments in the same direction (Pereira & Saito, 2015).

As noted by Bellof and Wehn (2018), estimation errors or parameter uncertainties caused by algorithmic methods use of statistics are areas of model risk that requires further investigation. Eastburn and Sharland (2017) asserts the growing risk can force banks out of business and eventually spill over negatively into the economy; this increase of risk can be prevented in a respectable risk culture that informs all financial risk-taking and managerial decisions. The public company scandals that led to the passing of SOX brought rapid changes, technological developments and complexities that highlighted the importance of effective internal control as a crucial element of the global business ecosystem (Aksoy & Mohammed, 2020). The need for effective internal control is a requirement in all business sectors which the company's management (including governing board) is responsible for the design, management and effectiveness of the internal control system (Aksoy & Mohammed, 2020). The control environment improves and becomes more efficient when manual process becomes automated. The automation of manual processes reduces human errors and allows employee more time to prepare and review their work without cutting corners.

There are some automated processes that relied on models to calculate risk had errors in their results; the design of those systems faced challenges that were unremediated that led to inaccuracies. Bellof and Wehn (2018) posits estimation and statistical errors from algorithmic methods generated inaccuracies; this presented challenges in capital and loss projections in the banks. Eastburn and Sharland (2017) state that the growing bank risk can force banks out of business and eventually spill over negatively into the economy, which this increase of risk can be prevented in a respectable risk culture that informs all financial risk-taking and managerial decisions. As such, the capability of being able to predict risk accurately is highly needed. Bank managers should implement the right internal controls systems, ensure performance as designed, and prioritize its importance as a vital part of an entity's administration framework (Aksoy & Mohammed, 2020). Allen et al. (2016) posit control activities enhanced through regulation requirements aim to contain systemic risk and maintain financial stability. The use of periodic risk and controls assessment is a key control activity that can be an effective risk reduction activity (Velez, 2020).

Conclusion

The increased risk in banks and public companies stemming from fraud, inaccuracies in reporting and significant losses has led to bankruptcies and negative spillovers into the economy. Global regulators have responded by passing laws to address these issues that place emphasis on the requirements of effective internal controls. In the United States, the law that addressed the internal controls requirements is documented in SOX 2002. This Act requires Public Company Accounting Oversight Board (PCAOB) provide independent oversight of auditors, external auditor independence/conflicts of interest, senior executives held responsible for accuracy and completeness of company's financial reports, internal controls to ensure accuracy of financial reports and audits to be performed on those controls, restoration of investor confidence through defining codes of conduct for securities analysts, Securities Exchange Commission authority to censure/bar securities professionals from practice, effects of consolidation of public accounting firms, credit rating agencies role in the operation of securities markets, securities violations and enforcement actions, criminal penalties for manipulation/destruction of financial records, protections for whistleblowers, corporate fraud and records tampering as criminal offenses with penalties and sentencing guidelines and penalties. Since the passing of SOX, many CEO and CFOs and employees participating in fraud have been prosecuted timely. While there have been improvements in reporting, there are still companies that struggle to implement effective controls that will assist them in meeting regulatory reporting requirement and the reduction of high risk. The control activities recommended by the panel of experts can bring efficiencies and improvements to the control environment. The important considerations identified can bolster effective internal control practices in an efficient manner by: (a) performance of periodic risk and controls assessment, (b) monthly/quarterly reporting over controls performance to include key performance/risk indicators, (c) strong governance and oversight committees, (d) timely reporting and escalation, (e) setting expectations for communication and reporting, (f) ensuring employees have time to recognize problems and follow procedures and not cut corners when they are under extreme pressure, (g) automation of manual processes that are prone to human errors, (h) establish priority training, (i) having a Risk Taxonomy. These considerations towards effective internal control practices may help reduce reporting inaccuracies and untimely reporting, and information disproportionateness which have caused significant losses. The failure to mitigate risk timely and lead to reputational damage, and regulatory findings. Academics, scholars, students, bank practitioners, regulators and accountants can gain understanding on internal control risk in banks/public companies and the use of effective internal control practices. Bank practitioners and regulators can leverage the suggestions made by the panel of experts composed of bank leaders to construct action plans and training programmes.

References

AB, M. (2018, May 30). Banks post highest ever annual losses: Eight banks reported losses of Rs53,000 crore in FY18. *DNA: Daily News & Analysis.*

Abdullah, A., Jan, S., & Malik, A. (2018). When 'Ameen' turns into a thief: A case of weak internal controls in a commercial bank. *Business and Economic Review*, *10*(2), 55–64.

Abiola, I., & Oyewole, A. T. (2013). Internal control system on fraud detection: Nigeria experience. *Journal of Accounting and Finance*, *13*(5), 141–152.

Abou-El-Sood, H. (2017). Corporate governance structure and capital adequacy: Implications to bank risk taking. *International Journal of Managerial Finance*, *13*(2), 165–185.

Act, S. O. (2002). *Sarbanes-Oxley Act. Washington DSarbanes-Oxley Act 2002, Sarbanes-Oxley Act.* Government Printing Office.

Aiyar, S., Calomiris, C. W., & Wieladek, T. (2015). Bank capital regulation: Theory, empirics, and policy. *IMF Economic Review*, *63*(4), 955–983.

Aksoy, T., & Mohammed, A. (2020). Assessing bank's internal control effectiveness: The case of Ghanaian listed banks. *International Journal of Research in Business and Social Science*, *9*(4), 196–206.

Al-Hawatmeh, O. (2021). The possibility of using balance scorecard (BSC) in evaluating the performance of internal control in Jordanian Commercial Banks (JCB). *International Journal of Information, Business and Management*, *13*(3), 178–189.

Al-Matari, Y., Saif Mohammed, S. A., & Al-Matari, E. (2017). Audit committee activities and the internal control system of commercial banks operating in Yemen. *International Review of Management and Marketing*, *7*(1).

Alampalli, S. (2013). Information infrastructure for systemic regulation. *Journal of Financial Regulation and Compliance*, *21*(3), 204–216.

Alexander, P., Fakhoury, R., Horn, T., Panjwani, W., & Roberts-Sklar, M. (2023). *Financial stability buy/sell tools: A gilt market case study.* Bank of England Quarterly Bulletin.

Aliaga-Díaz, R., & Olivero, M. P. (2012). Do bank capital requirements amplify business cycles? Bridging the gap between theory and empirics. *Macroeconomic Dynamics*, *16*(3), 358–395.

Allen, F., Goldstein, I., Jagtiani, J., & Lang, W. W. (2016). Enhancing prudential standards in financial regulations. *Journal of Financial Services Research*, *49*(2–3), 133–149.

Allison, J. A. (2017). The impact of monetary and regulatory policy on Main Street banking. *Cato Journal*, *37*(2), 207–215.

Álvarez-Franco, P. B., & Restrepo-Tobón, D. A. (2016). Managerial efficiency and failure of U.S. commercial banks during the 2007–2009 financial crisis: Was this time different? *Ecos de Economía*, *20*(43), 4–22.

Anouar, R. M., Fakhri, I., & Salem, B. (2017). Operational risk management in tunisian banks. *IUP Journal of Operations Management*, *16*(3), 39–60.

Arner, D. W., Barberis, J., & Buckley, R. P. (2017). FinTech, RegTech, and the reconceptualization of financial regulation. *Northwestern Journal of International Law & Business*, *37*(3), 371–413.

Arnold, M., & Goff, S. (2014, May 06). Hedge funds chase assets as bad banks cut losses: BANKS. *Financial Times*.

Badar, N. A., Arshad, S., & Liang, Y. (2017). Trade openness and bank risk-taking behavior: Evidence from emerging economies. *Journal of Risk and Financial Management*, *10*(3).

Baker Akram, F. J., Zaqeeba, N., Al-Jarrah, M. F. M., Abdalla Mohammad, A. B., & Almatarneh, Z. (2023). The mediating effect of the internal control system on the relationship between the accounting information system and employee performance in Jordan Islamic Banks. *Economies*, *11*(3), 77.

Baker, C., Cummings, C., & Jagtiani, J. (2017). The impacts of financial regulations: Solvency and liquidity in the post-crisis period. *Journal of Financial Regulation and Compliance*, *25*(3), 253–270.

Baker, H. K., & Filbeck, G.. (2015). Risk management: A panel discussion. *Journal of Applied Finance*, *25*(1), 46–57.

Baradaran, M. (2014). Regulation by hypothetical. *Vanderbilt Law Review*, *67*(5), 1247–1326.

Barr, M. S. (2017). Financial reform: Making the system safer and fairer. *RSF: The Russell Sage Foundation Journal of the Social Sciences*, *3*(1), 2–18.

Bellof, T., & Wehn, C. S. (2018). On the treatment of model risk in the internal capital dequacy assessment process. *Journal of Applied Finance and Banking*, *8*(4), 1–15.

Berger, A. N., Curti, F., Mihov, A., & Sedunov, J. (2018). Operational risk is more systemic than you think: Evidence from US bank holding companies. https://papers.ssrn.com/sol3/papers.cfm?abstract_id=3210808

Bezo, A., & Dibra, R. (2023). Financial system audit and governance after the financial crisis: Acces la success. *Calitatea*, *24*(194), 403–408.

Bezzina, F., Grima, S., & Mamo, J. (2014). Risk management practices adopted by financial firms in Malta. *Managerial Finance*, *40*(6), 587–612.

Biljanovska, B. (2016). Aligning market discipline and financial stability: A more gradual shift from contingent convertible capital to bail-in measures. *European Business Organization Law Review*, *17*(1–2), 105–135.

Black, L., Krainer, J., & Nichols, J. (2017). From origination to renegotiation: A comparison of portfolio and securitized commercial real estate loans. *The Journal of Real Estate Finance and Economics*, *55*(1), 1–31.

Boora, K. K., & Kavita. (2018). Implementation of basel III norms in banking industry: A review of empirical literature. *IUP Journal of Bank Management*, *17*(3), 7–24.

Bressan, S. (2017). Effects from the parent's exposure to subsidiaries inside bank holding companies (BHCs). *Journal of Banking Regulation*, *18*(2), 132–148.

Canniffe, M. (2002, February 08). Bank's losses leave countless questions unanswered: [City edition]. *Irish Times*.

Chang, Y., & Talley, D. A. (2017). Bank risk in a decade of low interest rates. *Journal of Economics and Finance*, *41*(3), 505–528.

Chawla, V. (2016). Workplace spirituality governance: Impact on customer orientation and salesperson performance. *Journal of Business & Industrial Marketing*, *31*(4), 498–506.

Chen, F., Zhu, J., & Wang, W. (2023). Overseas compliance risk prevention for multinational corporations in a law and economics perspective: Empirical evidence from Chinese MNCs. *Multinational Business Review*, *31*(1), 136–156.

Chowdhury, E. K. (2021). Does internal control influence financial performance of commercial banks? Evidence from Bangladesh. *South Asian Journal of Management*, *28*(1), 59–77.

Coffee, J. C., Jr. (2018). The retreat from systemic risk regulation: What explains it? (and why it was predictable). *Réalités Industrielles*, *80–90*, 115–116.

Cowie, I. (2012, November 03). Can we ever recover our bank losses?: Anyone who bought bank shares before the crisis has made punishing losses. But what are their prospects now, asks Ian Cowie. *The Daily Telegraph*.

Crabb, J. (2018). *CCAR results highlight Fed's lack of transparency*. International Financial Law Review.

Crawford, J. (2017). *Lesson unlearned?: Regulatory reform and financial stability in the Trump Administration*. Columbia Law Review Online, Forthcoming; UC Hastings Research Paper No. 242.

Dandapani, K., Lawrence, E. R., & Patterson, F. M. (2017). The effect of holding company affiliation on bank risk and the 2008 financial crisis. *Studies in Economics and Finance*, *34*(1), 105–121.

Darayseh, M., & Chazi, A. (2018). Bank specifics, economics environment, and agency theory: Determinants of banking performance in GCC. *The Journal of Developing Areas*, *52*(4), 199–212.

Davies, P. (2015). The fall and rise of debt: Bank capital regulation after the crisis. *European Business Organization Law Review*, *16*(3), 491–512.

de Jongh, E., de Jongh, R., de Jongh, D., & Gary, v. V. (2013). A review of operational risk in banks and its role in the financial crisis. *South African Journal of Economic and Management Sciences*, *16*(4), 364–382.

Denev, A., & Mutnikas, Y. (2016). A formalized, integrated and visual approach to stress testing. *Risk Management*, *18*(4), 189–216.

Deos, S., Bullio, O., de Mendonça, A., & Rosa, R. (2015). Banking-system transformations after the crisis and their impacts on regulation. *Journal of European Economic History*, *44*(2), 77–111.

Dowd, K., & Hutchinson, M. (2016). Learning the right lessons from the financial crisis. *Cato Journal*, *36*(2), 393–413.

Duncan, P. (2021). A methodology for enterprise-wide risk assessment in small banks and credit union. *Journal of Money Laundering Control*, *24*(2), 374–395.

Eastburn, R. W., & Sharland, A. (2017). Risk management and managerial mindset. *The Journal of Risk Finance*, *18*(1), 21–47.

Egly, P. V., Escobari, D., & Johnk, D. W. (2016). The impact of government intervention on the stabilization of domestic financial markets and on U.S. banks' asset composition. *Journal of Economics and Finance*, *40*(4), 683–713.

Eldridge, E., & Lynch, D. (1995, February 27). Markets reel after British bank's losses: [FINAL edition]. *USA Today*. (Pre-1997 Fulltext).

Erten, B., & Ocampo, J. A. (2017). Macroeconomic effects of capital account regulations. *IMF Economic Review*, *65*(2), 193–240.

Ertürk, I. (2016). Financialization, bank business models and the limits of post-crisis bank regulation. *Journal of Banking Regulation*, *17*(1–2), 60–72.

Fadun, O. S., & Oye, D. (2020). Impacts of operational risk management on financial performance: A case of commercial banks in Nigeria. *International Journal of Finance & Banking Studies*, *9*(1), 22-35.

Fahey, C. (2016). Are we ready for the next financial crisis? *Fordham Journal of Corporate and Financial Law*, *21*(2), 232–294.

Fischer, D. (2015). Dodd-Frank's failure to address to address CFTC oversight of self-regulatory organization rulemaking. *Columbia Law Review*, *115*(1), 69–125.

Forrer, A. S., & Forrer, D. A. (2015). Analysis of the relationship between economic cycle swings and adoption rate models of financial innovation diffusion. *Journal of Business & Economics Research*, *13*(2), 103.

Frank, P. H. (1991, December 10). Losses pile up at state banks 2 banks account for most losses in 3rd quarter: [Final edition]. *Evening Sun*.

Frank Nana, K. O., Kaur, M., & Nissar, A. R. (2023). Evaluating the impact of internal control systems on organizational effectiveness. *LBS Journal of Management & Research*, *21*(1), 135–154.

Fukuda, S. (2016). Bank's capital requirements in the business cycle: A DSGE analysis with a news shock. *Journal of Applied Finance and Banking*, *6*(3), 115–128.

Gastón, A. G., & Schumacher, I. (2017). An empirical study on the impact of basel III standards on banks' default risk: The case of Luxembourg. *Journal of Risk and Financial Management*, *10*(2).

Gatzert, N., & Schmit, J. (2016). Supporting strategic success through enterprise-wide reputation risk management. *The Journal of Risk Finance*, *17*(1), 26–45.

Ghosh, T. P. (2021). Compliance risk management in indian banks: Analysis of regulatory actions. *Prajnan*, *50*(1), 73–99.

Glasserman, P., & Tangirala, G. (2016). Are the federal reserve's stress test results predictable? *Journal of Alternative Investments*, *18*(4), 82–97.

Goldberg, M. (2017). Much of model risk does not come from any model. *Journal of Structured Finance*, *23*(1), 32–37.

Gordon, J. N., & Ringe, W. (2015). Bank resolution in the European Banking Union: A transatlantic perspective on what it would take. *Columbia Law Review*, *115*(5), 1297–1369.

Gorton, G. (2015). Stress for success: A review of timothy geithner's financial crisis memoir. *Journal of Economic Literature*, *53*(4), 975–995.

Greenwood, R., Stein, J. C., Hanson, S. G., & Sunderam, A. (2017). Strengthening and streamlining bank capital regulation. *Brookings Papers on Economic Activity*, 479–565.

Gregory, K., & Hambusch, G. (2015). Factors driving risk in the US banking industry. *International Journal of Managerial Finance*, *11*(3), 388–410.

Gullo, K., & Kalish, D. E. (1995, September 27). Bond trader charged in bank's $1.1B loss; Daiwa bank worker doctored records, U.S. officials allege: [Final edition]. *The Ottawa Citizen*.

Guynn, R. D. (2010). The global financial crisis and proposed regulatory reform. *Brigham Young University Law Review*, *2010*(2), 421–513.

Haddad, M. M., & Hakim, S. (2017). Can gulf banks pass the CCAR stress tests? *The Journal of Applied Business and Economics*, *19*(1), 44–59.

Hagen, R., Fritz-Morgenthal, S., & Posch, P. N. (2020). Whale watching on the trading floor: Unravelling collusive rogue trading in banks. *Journal of Business Ethics*, *165*(4), 633–657.

Hale, B. (2016). The political economy of financial regulation policies following the global crisis. *International Journal of Economics and Financial Issues*, *6*(2).

Hamed, R. (2023). The role of internal control systems in ensuring financial performance sustainability. *Sustainability*, *15*(13), 10206.

Handorf, W. C. (2017). Regulatory ratios, CDS spreads, and credit ratings in a favorable economic environment. *Journal of Banking Regulation*, *18*(3), 268–285.

Hanke, S. H., & Sekerke, M. (2017). Bank regulation as monetary policy: Lessons from the great recession. *Cato Journal*, *37*(2), 385–405.

Helena, H. A., & Madsen, D. Ø. (2021). Developing a maturity model for the compliance function of investment firms: A preliminary case study from Norway. *Administrative Sciences*, *11*(4), 109.

Hemrit, W., & Arab, M. B. (2013). The major sources of operational risk and the potential benefits of its management. *The Journal of Operational Risk*, *7*(4), 71–92.

Herr, H. (2016). After the financial crisis: Reforms and reform options for finance, regulation and institutional structure. *Journal of Economics Bibliography*, *3*(2).

Herring, R. J. (2016). Less really can be more: Why simplicity & comparability should be regulatory objectives. *Atlantic Economic Journal*, *44*(1), 33-50.

Hideaki, S., & Naoki, W. (2021). Earnings quality and internal control in bank-dominated corporate governance. *Asian Business & Management*, *20*(2), 188–220.

Higgins, H. N. (2012). Learning internal controls from a fraud case at bank of China. *Issues in Accounting Education*, *27*(4), 1171–1192.

Hogan, T. L., & Meredith, N. R. (2016). Risk and risk-based capital of U.S. bank holding companies. *Journal of Regulatory Economics*, *49*(1), 86–112.

Izhar, H., & Asutay, M. (2010). A theoretical analysis of the operational risk framework in Islamic Banks. *IIUM Journal of Economics and Management*, *18*(1), 73–113.

Jacobs, M. (2016). Stress testing and a comparison of alternative methodologies for scenario generation. *Journal of Applied Finance and Banking*, *6*(6), 123–156.

Johnson, A. M. (2015). Legislation induced organizational inefficiency: The case of the federal reserve and the Dodd-Frank. *International Journal of Organization Theory and Behavior*, *18*(4), 434–453.

Kapinos, P., & Mitnik, O. A. (2016). A top-down approach to stress-testing banks. *Journal of Financial Services Research*, *49*(2–3), 229–264.

Kaur, M., & Kapoor, S. (2015). Risk-based capital regulation and bank behaviour: A critical review of literature from 1990 to 2013. *Prajnan*, *44*(1), 29–52.

Kavassalis, P., Stieber, H., Breymann, W., Saxton, K., & Gross, F. J. (2018). An innovative RegTech approach to financial risk monitoring and supervisory reporting. *The Journal of Risk Finance*, *19*(1), 39–55.

Khalil, F., & Hasan, M. A. (2020). Identification of fintech driven operational risk events. *Journal of the Research Society of Pakistan*, *57*(1), 75.

Kim, H. (2016). Financial regulation and supervision in corporate governance of banks. *The Journal of Corporation Law*, *41*(3), 707–726.

Ko, C., Lee, P., & Anandarajan, A. (2019). The impact of operational risk incidents and moderating influence of corporate governance on credit risk and firm performance. *International Journal of Accounting and Information Management*, *27*(1), 96–110.

Kolari, J. W., & Ivan, P. S. (2017). Systemic risk measurement in banking using self-organizing maps. *Journal of Banking Regulation*, *18*(4), 338–358.

Labonte, M. (2013). Systemically important or "too big to fail" financial institutions. *Journal of Current Issues in Finance, Business and Economics*, *6*(1), 39–96.

Lai, K. (2018). *HMKA: Regtech is one answer to increase in regulation*. International Financial Law Review.

Laiola, R. (2015). Tier 1 capital ratios: The regulation of risk behavior continues. *Academy of Accounting and Financial Studies Journal*, *19*(3), 165–187.

Le, H. T. T, Narayanan, R. P., & Van Vo, L. (2016). Has the effect of asset securitization on bank risk taking behavior changed? *Journal of Financial Services Research*, *49*(1), 39–64.

Leahy, J. (2000, January 10). Indonesian central bank's losses may be higher: [London edition]. *Financial Times*.

Lee, L. (2015). Successfully navigating CCAR and DFAST. *Journal of Structured Finance*, *21*(3), 51–55.

Lin, J., Chen, S., & Fu-Wei, H. (2018). Bank interest margin, multiple shadow banking activities, and capital regulation. *International Journal of Financial Studies*, *6*(3).

Lui, A. (2011). Multiple principal-agent problems in securitisation. *The Poznan University of Economics Review*, *11*(2), 47–72.

Maksimovic, S., Vlaskovic, V., Jovic, D., & Zivanovic, N. (2023). *Internal audit in the function of corporate management in the public sector of Serbia*. Varazdin Development and Entrepreneurship Agency (VADEA).

Malpezzi, S. (2017). Residential real estate in the U.S. financial crisis, the great recession, and their aftermath. *Jing Ji Lun Wen Cong Kan*, *45*(1), 5–56.

Mamonov, S., & Benbunan-Fich, R. (2017). What can we learn from past mistakes? Lessons from data mining the fannie mae mortgage portfolio. *Journal of Real Estate Research*, *39*(2), 235–262.

Masera, R., & Mazzoni, G. (2016). On the non-neutrality of the financing policy and the capital regulation of banking firms. *Studies in Economics and Finance*, *33*(4), 466–487.

Maxfield, S., & Sousa, M. D. (2015). The global financial crisis and banking sector resilience. *Journal of Banking Regulation*, *16*(4), 265–288.

McConnell, P. (2012). Systemic operational risk: Smoke and mirrors. *The Journal of Operational Risk*, *7*(3), 119–164.

Mcmillan, D. G., & Mcmillan, F. J. (2016). US bank market structure: Evolving nature and implications. *Journal of Financial Services Research*, *50*(2), 187–210.

Meager, L. (2017). *Regtech must serve a purpose*. International Financial Law Review.

Mohamed, A. R. (2015). Effective regulatory regimes: A comparative analysis of GCC financial regulators. *Journal of Financial Regulation and Compliance*, *23*(1), 2-17.

Montagano, C. P. (2012). The global crackdown on insider trading: A silver lining to the "great recession". *Indiana Journal of Global Legal Studies*, *19*(2), 575–598.

Motel, L. (2016). Increasing diversity through goal-setting in corporate social responsibility reporting. *Equality, Diversity and Inclusion: An International Journal*, *35*(5), 328–349.

Nabil Ahmed, M. S. (2024). The moderating role of corporate governance on the associations of internal audit and its quality with the financial reporting quality: The case of Yemeni Banks. *Journal of Risk and Financial Management*, *17*(3), 124.

Newlands, E., & Makortoff, K. (2018, April 27). Setbacks see Barclays swing to Q1 loss: Bank's £236m loss comes amid PPI charges and DOJ settlement. *The Scotsman*.

Nisha, N. (2016). Global financial crisis: Exploring the special role of U.S. banks and regulations. *International Journal of Banking, Risk and Insurance*, *4*(1), 53–63.

Nitescu, D. C., & Duna, F. A. (2016). Liquidity management and the banking lending mechanism. *Revista de Management Comparat International*, *17*(4), 403–413.

Noreen, U., Alamdar, F., & Tariq, T. (2016). Capital buffers and bank risk: Empirical study of adjustment of Pakistani banks. *International Journal of Economics and Financial Issues*, *6*(4).

O'Sullivan, J., Mamun, A., & Hassan, M. K. (2016). The relationship between board characteristics and performance of bank holding companies: Before and during the financial crisis. *Journal of Economics and Finance*, *40*(3), 438–471.

Ong, L. L., & Pazarbasioglu, C. (2014). Credibility and crisis stress testing. *International Journal of Financial Studies*, *2*(1), 15–81.

Osterloh, M., & Frey, B. S. (2000). Motivation, knowledge transfer, and organizational forms. *Organization Science*, *11*(5), 538–550.

Pakhchanyan, S. (2016). Operational risk management in financial institutions: A literature review. *International Journal of Financial Studies*, *4*(4), 20.

Parnes, D. (2014). Assimilating operational risks in common trading systems. *The Journal of Operational Risk*, *9*(1), 57–73.

Paulet, E. (2016). Regulation and stability of banks in large-scale crises: An historical approach. *Journal of European Economic History*, *45*(1), 99–118.

Pereira, J. A. M., & Saito, R. (2015). Coordination of capital buffer and risk profile under supervision of central bank (coordenação entre capital buffer e perfil de risco sob supervisão do banco central). *Revista Brasileira De Finanças*, *13*(1), 73–101.

Petersen, M. A., Senosi, M. C., Mukuddem-Petersen, J., Mulaudzi, M. P., & Schoeman, I. M. (2009). Did bank capital regulation exacerbate the subprime mortgage crisis? *Discrete Dynamics in Nature and Society*, https://doi.org/10.1155/2009/742968

Petitjean, M. (2013). Bank failures and regulation: A critical review. *Journal of Financial Regulation and Compliance*, *21*(1), 16–38.

Pfeifer, L., Holub, L., Pikhart, Z., & Hodula, M. (2017). Leverage ratio and its impact on the resilience of the banking sector and efficiency of macroprudential policy. *Finance a Uver*, *67*(4), 277–299.

Polizzi, S., & Scannella, E. (2023). Continuous auditing in public sector and central banks: A framework to tackle implementation challenges. *Journal of Financial Regulation and Compliance*, *31*(1), 40–59.

Pollick, M., Skof, B., & Kobal, A. (2016). Protecting public interest in financial crisis. *Lex Localis*, *14*(1), 19–32.

Prasch, R. E. (2012). The Dodd-Frank Act: Financial reform or business as usual? *Journal of Economic Issues*, *46*(2), 549–556.

PRIMER. (2018). *PRIMER: Operational risk – Prudential regulation perspective.* International Financial Law Review.

Rahim, N. F. A., Ahmed, E. R., & Faeeq, M. K. (2018). Internal control system and perceived operational risk management in Malaysian conventional banking industry. *Global Business and Management Research*, *10*(1), 135–149.

Rao, N. (2010). A modest proposal: Abolishing agency independence in Free Enterprise Fund v PCAOB. *Fordham Law Review*, *79*, 2541.

Redo, M. (2015). The importance of prudential regulations in the process of transmitting monetary policy to economy. *Copernican Journal of Finance and Accounting*, *4*(2), 145–158.

Repousis, S., Petros, L., & Veli, V. (2019). An investigation of the fraud risk and fraud scheme methods in Greek commercial banks. *Journal of Money Laundering Control*, *22*(1), 53–61.

Robertson, T. J., & Sullivan, L. L. (2009). Bad boys of business make for bad business decisions: A study in ethics. *Southern Journal of Business and Ethics*, *1*, 87–100.

Salameh, R. S. (2019). What is the impact of internal control system on the quality of banks' financial statements in Jordan? *Academy of Accounting and Financial Studies Journal*, *23*(5), 1–10.

Sarin, N., & Summers, L. H. (2016). Understanding bank risk through market measures. *Brookings Papers on Economic Activity*, 57–127.

Schenk, C. (2017). Rogue trading at lloyds bank international, 1974: Operational risk in volatile markets. *Business History Review*, *91*(1), 105–128.

Schwarcz, D., & Zaring, D. (2017). Regulation by threat: Dodd-Frank and the nonbank problem. *University of Chicago Law Review*, *84*(4), 1813–1881.

Sepdiningtyas, R., & Santoso, C. B. (2017). The influence of leader-member exchange on individual performance: The roles of work engagement as a mediating variable and co-workers support as a moderating variable. *Review of Integrative Business and Economics Research*, *6*(4), 285–305.

Shannon, K. (2001, November 28). Bad loans bite bank; credit losses at bank of Montreal total more than $500M: [Final edition]. *Windsor Star*.

Shi, X. C., & Wang, S. (2014). The application of information technology in bank accounting internal control risk. *Applied Mechanics and Materials*, *631–632*, 1291-1294. 1291.

Shorter, G., Murphy, E. V., & Miller, R. S. (2012). Jp Morgan trading losses: Implications for the volcker rule and other regulation. *Journal of Current Issues in Finance, Business and Economics*, *5*(3), 317–347.

Stein, G. (2002, April 24). Bank losses in Argentina grow by 60%: International banks have already taken an US$8.5-billion hit and see more losses ahead: Six international banks (Toronto/Late edition headline.); Bank losses in Argentina grow by 60%: Six international banks: More losses to come as total reaches US$8.5-billion (All but Toronto/Late edition headline.): [National edition]. *National Post*.

Stigliano, A. L. (2011). *Sarbanes-Oxley and corporate Greed*. UConn Library.

Stubbs, W., & Higgins, C. (2018). Stakeholders' perspectives on the role of regulatory reform in integrated reporting. *Journal of Business Ethics*, *147*(3), 489–508.

Suresh, A., & Monalisa, M. A. (2024). Downfall of credit Suisse impacting the bancassurance and stock instability. *Journal of Economic Development, Management, IT, Finance, and Marketing*, *16*(1), 9–27.

Tanda, A. (2015). The effects of bank regulation on the relationship between capital and risk. *Comparative Economic Studies*, *57*(1), 31–54.

Thomsen, L. C., & Norman, D. (2008) Sarbanes-Oxley turns six: An enforcement perspective. *Journal of Business & Technology Law*, *3*, 393.

Tourigny, L., Dougan, W. L., Washbush, J., & Clements, C. (2003). Explaining executive integrity: Governance, charisma, personality and agency. *Management Decision*, *41*(10), 1035–1049.

Trendowski, J., & Rustambekov, E. (2017). Risk taking and bank failure before and after the onset of the financial crisis - A decade in review. *The Journal of Applied Business and Economics*, *19*(8), 79–93.

Tung, F. (2011). Pay for banker performance: Structuring executive compensation for risk regulation. *Northwestern University Law Review*, *105*(3), 1205–1251.

Velez, S. (2020). *Building consensus on the capital regulation practices of senior bank managers*. Doctoral dissertation. Walden University.

Viljanen, M. (2016). Making banks on a global scale: Management-based regulation as agencement. *Indiana Journal of Global Legal Studies*, *23*(2), 425–454.

Walaa, W. E., & Tucker, J. (2016). Bank regulation and stock market stability across countries. *Journal of Financial Regulation and Compliance*, *24*(4), 402–419.

Walker, D. A., Dammeyer, E., & Lee, E. (2017). Banks' Dodd-Frank costs vs. earnings on reserves. *Journal of Accounting and Finance*, *17*(8), 10–28.

Wall, L. D. (2017). Recent changes in US regulation of large foreign banking organizations. *Journal of Financial Regulation and Compliance*, *25*(3), 318–332.

Wan, J. S. (2016). Systematically important asset managers: Perspectives on Dodd-Frank's systemic designation mechanism. *Columbia Law Review*, *116*(3), 805–841.

Yuan, Y. (2017). Can U.S. banks and insurers achieve benefits promised by financial integration? *Journal of Accounting and Finance*, *17*(4), 110–129.

Index

Printed and bound by CPI Group (UK) Ltd, Croydon, CR0 4YY

24/08/2026

14947975-0001